Barnstormers & Daredevils

Books by K. C. Tessendorf

Look Out! Here Comes the Stanley Steamer
Kill the Tsar!
Uncle Sam in Nicaragua
Barnstormers & Daredevils

K. C. TESSENDORF

BARNSTORMERS
&
DAREDEVILS

JUL 2 6 1989

CONTRA COSTA COUNTY LIBRARY

3 1901 01166 8904

ATHENEUM   1988   NEW YORK

Photo Credits

National Air and Space Museum, Smithsonian Institution: title page,
    5, 8, 13, 24, 27, 32, 35, 37, 38–39, 40 (top), 41, 49, 54, 55,
    58, 64, 65, 67, 71, 77, 79, 83
National Archives: 10, 11
National Aviation Museum, Ottawa, Canada: 16, 30
Collection of the Minnesota Historical Society: 43
Lindbergh Picture Collection, Yale University Library: 47
American Hall of Aviation History Collection, Northrop University: 56,
    59, 60, 80, 81
Harry Ransom Humanities Research Center at the University of Texas
    at Austin: 69, 73
From Everybody's Aviation Guide by Victor W. Page (1928): 15
From "Some Real Facts About Parachutes," by George Waite, Aviation
    Mechanics, July 1930: 34, 61
Courtesy Mr. Harold D. Hoekstra, Private Collection: 23

Copyright © 1988 by K. C. Tessendorf
All rights reserved. No part of this book may be reproduced
or transmitted in any form or by any means, electronic or
mechanical, including photocopying, recording, or by any
information storage and retrieval system, without permission
in writing from the publisher.

Atheneum
Macmillan Publishing Company, 866 Third Avenue, New York, NY 10022
Collier Macmillan Canada, Inc.

First Edition
10 9 8 7 6 5 4 3 2 1

Library of Congress Cataloging-in-Publication Data

Tessendorf, K. C.   Barnstormers and daredevils.

Bibliography: p. 84
Includes index.
SUMMARY: A history of barnstorming in America, with an
ample number of anecdotes about the dangerous acrobatics
and stunts performed by thrill-seeking exhibition flyers,
mostly ex-military pilots, especially during the 1920's.
1. Stunt flying—Juvenile literature. 2. Stunt flying.
3. Aeronautics—History. I. Title
TL711.S8.T47 1988   797.5'4   87-15194
ISBN 0-689-31346-2

Title page: Group portrait of Gates Air Circus personnel
with part of their aerial fleet in the background.

I guess we were a strange lot, those of us who flew those old traps every Sunday at the field. Maybe we were a sort of mixture of the cowhand of the Old West, the hot-rod driver of today, and the real gypsy. We thought we were as free as the birds when we got in the air, just the way the oldtime cowhand thought he was as free as a coyote. We deliberately missed death by inches, just like the hot-rod driver of today. And we played the suckers wherever we could find them, which meant roaming the face of the earth like a gypsy.

Slats Rodgers,
Barnstormer

For Marlis, who made it possible

CONTENTS

Barnstormers & Daredevils

CHAPTER

I

A Roar Out of the Twenties

IMAGINE a blue June day in America's midsection, the million square miles of level farmlands lying between the Appalachian and the Rocky mountains. High in that summer sky, a big brown biplane is roaring on its way, an unusual sight to see over the countryside of sixty years ago. Down below maybe a hundred screen doors have banged along the airplane's way as rural folk, especially kids, scooted outside to squint up at the noisy passing of the barnstormer:

The old bus was humming along sweetly at a sixty-mile air speed, which meant a rate of forty-five miles an hour in relation to the ground, for she was bucking a fifteen-mile breeze. I slumped back in the rear cockpit, handling the controls easily and comfortably as I drifted into that drowsy, wholly content state of mind the pilot so often experiences when the motor holds its even rhythm and the bumps come soft and seldom. Once in a while I'd lean over the edge of the fuselage to scan the flat checkered prairie country for bearings, or to watch a toy train crawling over its narrow tracks 2000 feet below, but chiefly I just rested and thought idly and regretfully about the card game that had cleaned me out the night before.

Then suddenly I heard the faint spit-spit and felt the miss in the motor that told me it was gasping for gas. I knew what was wrong. Before taking off that morning I had drained the water from the carburetor wells, so the trouble wasn't there. The gas tank must be empty. Of course I had poured in what

I thought would be sufficient fuel, but, confound it, I hadn't counted on that fifteen-mile head wind. Anyhow, there I was, 2000 feet in the air, twenty miles from my objective, out of gas—and broke.

There was nothing much to worry about immediately. I was flying one of the old JN4 training planes—the famous Jennies of the army camps—and I knew she had a gliding ratio of seven to one, which meant that since I was 2000 feet high, I could alight on any comparatively level field within a rough radius of 14,000 feet. I spotted one that I could reach easily—a stubble field by its lightish-brown color—not too far from the paved state road that wound like a twisting bit of white baby ribbon through the softly shaded green-and-brown farm lands. So I pulled the throttle back and nosed down, making a wide sweeping spiral which I hoped would attract attention.

The flying wires screamed their first high note as they cut the air in the speed of that glide, then changed to the low-toned landing song as I leveled off a few feet above the ground to make as pretty a three-point landing, square into the wind, as anyone could wish to see. Then I rolled a bit nearer the road and waited—wishing that my hard-boiled instructor back in 1917 had seen that landing; wishing that I had a few gallons of gas . . .

Happily, a forced landing out in rural America could be fortunate, for airplanes were still rare to see, to touch, to ride in during the 1920s, that time when people thought that they would soon get rich investing in the stock market, and free spirits, including the barnstormers, started freewheeling through life.

I hadn't long to wait. Almost before I had cut my ignition the farmer came boiling out from his house 500 yards away. He started yelling before he left the doorstep and kept it up as he climbed three rail fences and jumped a ditch on his way to me. Finally he reached hearing distance.

"What are you doing in my field?" he bawled.

I wanted to tell him that I had come down to pick a four-leaf clover, but I decided to save my wisecracks.

"Tank's dry," I reported. "Where's there a garage round here?"

After he saw that my tail skid had only scratched the surface of his ground, and that I hadn't upset the rotation of crops, he calmed down. But he was still hoarse when he told me I'd find a filling station half a mile up the road. I suspected as much. That's why I always followed the state roads frequented by motorists when I was flying cross country.

I set that noisy tiller of the soil to watch the plane, and footed it, flying togs and all, up the pike. The ship was safe with him, so I didn't hurry. Besides, I wanted to give him plenty of time to swank around the old Jenny and to tell his

"Fill her up with gas and oil," I said, "and I'll give you a ride for nothing." Art Goebels, one of the best-known stunt flyers of the period.

neighbors and perhaps a few curious motorists all about it. I hoped to do business with them later. But just now I had a more pressing problem.

The garageman was waiting as I swaggered up rubbing a couple of thin dimes together in my pocket to make them feel less lonely. He had seen, as I hoped he would, that trick spiral landing.

"That your aeryoplane?" he demanded.

"Yes," I replied. "I came down to give you a hop. Only ten bucks."

"Nope, don't want to ride in one of them things. Air's too soft and the ground's too hard. Besides it ain't worth ten dollars."

"Five dollars," I tempted him, "and I'll throw in a loop."

He began to weaken. Finally I broached the proposition I had planned from the beginning.

"Fill her up with gas and oil," I said, "and I'll give you a ride for nothing."

That won him. I drained the sump and put in fresh oil—for the old stuff was getting pretty thin—then filled the tank. It wasn't high-test gas, but it would do. After I had given the garageman his promised hop, I took up the farmer and two of his friends at five dollars each, then I flew away. My troubles were over. I was all set with gas and oil and money to take me to the county fair at Homburg, where I was sure to find plenty of passenger-carrying trade.

For I was gypsying the Jenny through the Corn Belt and had to snatch off my profits—and my upkeep—where I could.

CHAPTER

2

War Surplus Daredevils

TO UNDERSTAND the free, crazy, do-it-yourself time of flying called "barnstorming," its beginnings in the first sixteen years of the aviation era must be told.

In 1903, the Wright Brothers launched a gasoline-engine powered flying machine into the wind at Kitty Hawk, North Carolina, that flew low, slow, and straight—very briefly. Learning how to turn in the air without crashing was the first thrilling fundamental of aviation. In following years, the Wrights built—at Dayton, Ohio—better powered, more maneuverable airplanes that ventured out on short cross-country flights. Soon Glenn Curtiss competed with them, as a designer and builder of original aircraft at his base in Hammondsport, New York. Yet these flying machines remained frail and undependable. They strained when carrying two persons.

The airplane of 1906 was only a flyable freak. People didn't believe in airplanes. They had to see. And there was big money to be collected while showing them. As late as 1910, promoters at Baltimore offered $5,000 to the first adventurer who'd dare to fly nonstop across that city. In 1980s values, that would be at least $35,000! So it's understandable that the Wrights and Curtiss rushed to establish rival air exhibition teams to tour the country and educate the American people.

Many folks didn't believe that man had flown in a machine, or ever would. But people would pay for the sake of their curiosity; to see the flying machine fraud. When the freak did fly as advertised, the public was impressed, but afterward would have easily turned to new attractions. The flying machine showmen kept luring them back by offering new thrills and dangerous aerial escapades. Fliers therefore became well-paid aerial daredevils. As long as they survived.

The famous fliers of that period are practically forgotten today: Walter Brookins, Eugene Ely, Charles Hamilton, Arch Hoxsey, John Moisant, Cal Rodgers, even "the incomparable Lincoln Beachey," the greatest daredevil of them all. Linc was the first American who flew a loop, conquered the deadly airplane spin, had BEACHEY painted in huge letters on his *top* wing so that folks would know it was he flying upside down. Linc dove his primitive biplane, in which he sat in open air in front of the lower wing, over Niagara Falls into the mists and emerged still flying.

Crowds were fascinated by Beachey's auto track races with Bar-

Airborne Lincoln Beachey in his Curtiss pusher races Barney Oldfield on the track below in 1914.

rney Oldfield, a famous racing car driver. Round and round the track they tore and zoomed, and sometimes, if the air was very stable, Linc would inch down until the plane's forward wheel just below his feet nearly touched the radiator cap of Oldfield's speeding racer. Beachey is reported as having stunted in the closest quarters ever; very briefly taking off and landing *inside* a building!

A string of lesser fliers died attempting to match Beachey stunts, and even the grand master retired for a time. Watching for death in the "fool killers" was an added excitement for many in the air exhibition crowds. Lincoln Beachey, knowing this well, rudely despised the spectators whose admission fees were making him rich. He continued to earn up to $1,000 a performance until he crashed in a *real* "death dive" (his crowd-gasper specialty) at San Francisco, before fifty thousand watchers, in 1915.

By that year the first boom in air exhibition flying was fading. Daily, World War I in Europe presented truly death-dealing air contests. Young British, French, and German fliers were engaged in one-on-one air combat in the sky, using the word "ace" to honor the military flier who personally destroyed five enemy aircraft.

Pilots like Canadian Billy Bishop, Frenchman Charles Nungesser, German Ernst Udet "shot down" many times five planes. The "Red Baron" Manfred von Richthofen topped them all with eighty kills for Germany. The airplane had progressed from an airborne freak to a deadly, flying gun platform.

Then, in 1917, the United States entered the World War, and suddenly there was a pressing need for young Americans to train as military pilots. Training fields appeared, the most famous on the flat plains of Texas, like Kelly Field at San Antonio.

Training at the start was a patch-up affair a great deal of the time, with few good instructors and training aircraft. To succeed, or even to survive, the student had to have great natural ability, plus a lot of luck. Gradually, conditions improved at the U.S. training fields. For one thing, many sturdy, often forgiving Curtiss JN-4D ("Jennies") training planes were delivered.

Also some real life-or-death air war tactics were introduced into

Student pilots at Kelly Field, Texas, during World War I.

the curriculum of flying, such as military aerobatics. In the beginning, such life-saving maneuvers had been forbidden by stuffy, naive U.S. brass hats as frivolous. But what did the students (and instructors) do when they were out of sight of the officers? They tangled in mock aerial "dog fights" and crazy stunting.

Most American pilots were still in training, or on the way to the Western Front when on November 11, 1918, the war was over. Immediately, there was an oversupply of military pilots at a time when the Army's Air Service needed to keep on only a few—after "the war to end wars." Fliers in France or Texas faced return to civilian life: back to finish college, work in an office, or join the family business. Most did so, some after hesitation. A minority refused to give up their romantic dreams.

There were nearly nine thousand men who had received some level of pilot training. Fewer than eight hundred, though, had experienced the real thing—air combat over the Western Front. Many American fliers felt cheated of the glory they had worked hard to prepare for. And though many returned to civilian life secretly relieved that they had survived a year or two aloft in flimsy, flammable "crates," there were others who were in love with flying.

When these hard-core fliers looked at civil aviation, they soon realized that America was the most backward major nation in that respect. Airlines were beginning, with government money, in Europe. But in the United States the distances, terrain, and weather were more of a problem, and there was no government support to build passenger aircraft or maintain airlines. There *was* an air-mail service, but at this time it was flown by army pilots. Hard-pressed by distance, weather, poor operating conditions and aircraft, the air-mail service's crashes were becoming notorious.

Anyway, organized aviation smacked of regulation and routine. Fly straight and on schedule. The war surplus daredevils had had their fill of army regulations. They wanted to keep their personal freedom intact in the sky; to get up and away to roam as they pleased. One factor favored their dreams. There were hundreds of war surplus airplanes—mostly Jennies—available at affordable prices.

A few hundred free spirits bought Jennies and set off to visit, thrill, and carry into the sky—for profit—the inhabitants of small-town America who had never seen a prewar air exhibition, or for that matter, even an airplane. These fliers were the true barnstormers, from an old expression of the theater about skipping through the countryside doing short-run shows. The gypsy fliers didn't earn much money doing their aerial "hand-springs" and many quit after a season. But some incurables somehow continued their freestyle aviation shows through many summers during the 1920s.

One of nine thousand American World War I pilots in training at Kelly Field.

CHAPTER

3

"Too Nice a Girl to Fight"

THESE FREEWHEELING aerial acrobats would never have risen from a runway or cow pasture without their partner, Jenny. Where did she come from, and what sort of plane was she?

The early attitude of the U.S. government toward military aviation was pinchpenny. When the World War started abroad in 1914, at least one American air showman owned a larger "air force" (he bombed Washington, D.C., one night with firecrackers!) than the U.S. Army. As late as 1916, when a dozen planes might be shot down in a day over the Western Front, the army's air branch could provide only eight unarmed airplanes to assist General Pershing in the Mexican bandit wars. They were early "Jennies," a type that would increase by the thousands as the most popular American aircraft built in quantity in the United States during the World War I era.

Jenny was the child of an accidental meeting in a London shop in 1913 between Glenn H. Curtiss, the American aircraft designer and manufacturer, and twenty-two-year-old B. Douglas Thomas, a talented employee in the design department of the British Sopwith company. Curtiss was seeking a "tractor" design aircraft. Tractor meant the engine in front with the propellor pulling the plane. Most American planes of the time were pushers; the engine and propellor were behind. Curtiss believed the tractor type to be the more efficient, and pilots agreed. Crashes were common, and it was a little better to have the engine in your lap afterward than on your neck!

Thomas had fresh ideas, and Curtiss, moving on to Paris that evening, paid Thomas's fare to go along so that they could continue their conversation. It was agreed that each, by common guidelines, would design an aircraft and that Curtiss would build both. Thomas, in England, drew up his Model J, and Curtiss his Model N in America. After looking over blueprints that Thomas mailed, Curtiss cabled him: "Come over." Thomas did, permanently. Both the J and N models were assembled and flight-tested. Then the best qualities of both were combined into the first JN—"Jenny."

In 1915, while World War I raged across the Atlantic in Europe, the United States ranked fourteenth in the world in military aircraft. Jenny was the only respectable, proven American plane, so a huge factory was built at Buffalo, New York, to manufacture Jennies for the Allies and the United States. Eventually it produced one hundred planes per month. After America entered the war, JN-4Ds, the commonest model, were built in many places and flew worldwide. About

Glenn Curtiss shows a pup how it's done in one of his early Curtiss pushers.

eight thousand were turned out during the war. After the armistice, the government was so slow in ending contracts that twenty-three hundred unneeded Jennys were manufactured! Each Jenny cost the government between $5,500 and $8,000.

America's aircraft did not win the air war over France. Jenny was "too nice a girl to fight." The JN-4D couldn't match the speed or altitude or maneuverability of the real warbirds, and Jenny never tried. It was on the training fields of the United States, Canada, England, France, and other nations that the "Model T of the air" excelled. A survey of American pilots flying in the 1920s reported that 95 percent had trained in, or flown in the JN-4D.

Jenny was strongly built to cope with the strains and bumps that inexperienced or clumsy pilots caused her. The JN-4D's frame, wings, and tail were fashioned from spars of spruce wood, and a bit of ash, crafted and assembled with care. The pieces were kept taut by a lacing of piano wire tightened by turnbuckles.

Several coats of varnish made Jenny's innards glisten. Then the aircraft frame was wrapped in cotton or linen cloth, afterward saturated with a flammable finish popularly called "dope" that, while drying, shrank the cloth wrap to drumhead tightness. Exterior wiring adjusted the top and lower wings and tail surfaces to the proper angles for flight.

Jenny was fairly large for the time: wingspan (upper) 43 feet, (lower) 33 feet, length 27 feet, height 10 feet, empty weight 1430 pounds. The useful load was figured as including 21 gallons of gasoline and two passengers, each averaging 165 pounds, in two in-line cockpits, the rear occupied by the pilot.

The JN-4D was somewhat underpowered by a so-so 90-horsepower OX-5 engine. It delivered 75 miles per hour top speed, but 60 to 65 mph was its preferred pace. The rate of climb was 200 feet per minute to a maximum altitude of 6,500 feet (but don't count on it). Jenny landed at 45 mph, bounced, and rolled . . . brakes hadn't been installed in airplanes yet. Skid loops set below the outer tips of the lower wings protected them from injury if the pilot had to swerve.

Jenny did not appreciate being manhandled, or provoked by

sloppy maneuvering. A typical reaction was to go off down to the left in a spin. Many early aviators crashed in spins until Beachey and others learned how to deal with their problem.

Yet the JN-4D was lenient and forgiving compared with scrappy, speedy warbirds like the French Nieuport, or the British Sopwith Camel. They were superb combat instruments that demanded life-or-death pilot skills of a high order. Jenny accepted the steady, mediocre flier along with the better ones.

When fliers swore at their Jennys, it was often for shortcomings of the OX-5 engine. Failure in flight occurred with a regularity that caused the prudent pilot to be always alert for available pastures. Fortunately, the JN-4D glided well, and its low speed helped out in hit-or-miss forced landings in small fields. Then the lament often was: "The #&%()! camshaft broke!" The OX-5 was also ill-famed for hesitancy. In an emergency, jamming on the throttle usually caused the

Dimensional drawings of Curtiss JN4 biplane. Jenny was the most widely used wartime training plane.

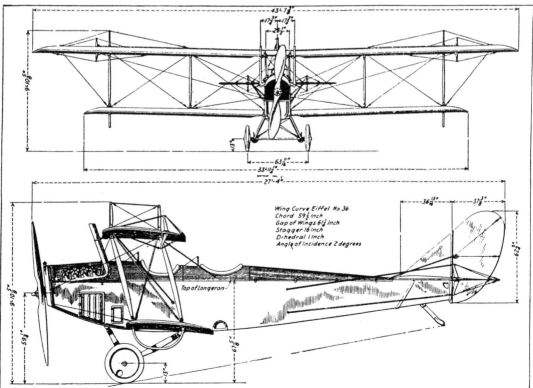

A daredevil stunts Jenny over the line of hangars on a Canadian training field.

engine to choke up. Barnstormers who could afford it installed a European engine, especially the Hispano-Suiza (Hisso) with 150 horsepower. Still, the old OX-5 was tamer than other American engines, which had a tendency to set themselves afire.

World War I ended in November 1918, and abruptly the government lost interest in military aviation. Thousands of airplanes in the United States, mostly Jennies, became war surplus objects. Some JN-4Ds were put on sale at about half their government purchase price. But then Canadian Jennies (Canucks) appeared on the market; Britain and France also sold Jennies in America. A buyer's market (too many planes) drove price down. By 1920, the advertised price for a first class JN-4D was $500; a junky one could be had for $250.

The government scrapped many aircraft, cutting the planes into large pieces. Major William B. Robertson bought the scrap for pennies and was able to restore for sale about 450 aircraft. Also, a flying school advertised a new idea: It cheaply purchased new JN-4Ds still in their crates and advertised a truly all-in-one price: Learn to fly; meanwhile learn about Jenny by building her; at graduation fly away in your own plane!

Out where the barnstormer headed was do-it-yourself territory. No airports existed, no repair shops, and usually no shelter for Jenny. Aircraft maintenance was totally up to the pilot. Some loved to overhaul an OX-5 engine, others shirked. Neglected airplanes crashed easily and often. The Curtiss quality plus owner upkeep kept Jenny in the air three to five years in primitive open-air circumstances. The JN-4D coped well as the barnstormer's partner. In and out of small or bumpy fields, carrying aloft for as little as a penny a pound the daring spectator, and showing the hicks aerobatic tricks.

LOOPING: The best-known stunt. The *inside* variety was a standard barnstormer feature. A shallow dive to pick up speed, back on the stick, and zoom upward arching back until upside down (where the OX-5 coughs in protest), then on down and around to level flight near the point of original climb. Sometimes the *inside* type was varied by a quarter roll and turn at completion to exit at a right angle. Centrifugal force kept pilot and plane parts together.

Flying through the inside loop.

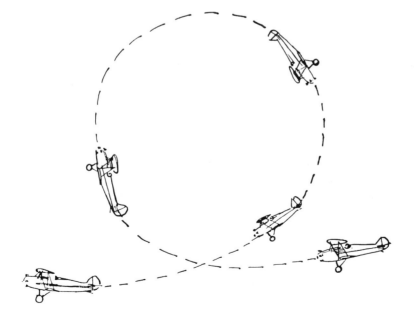

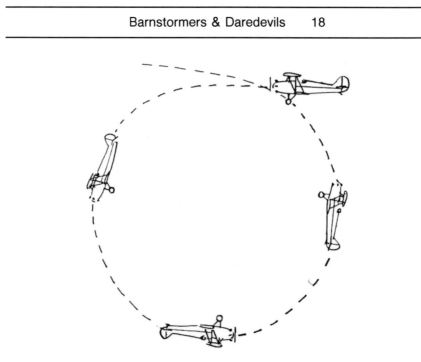

Centrifugal force pushing outward made the outside loop too tough for Jenny.

Doing the big O on the *outside* was decidedly the hard way, and not performed by barnstormers in Jennies. Instead of pressing together, the force pulled and separated pilot and plane, a difficult and dangerous stunt in aircraft of that era, and in fact not done in the United States until 1927, when Jimmie Doolittle performed it in an army pursuit plane, a Curtiss Hawk.

ROLLS: Rolling sideways in level flight was done in various ways: *Slow* rolls reduced the speed of turning; in a *half* roll, the pilot halted the plane briefly at the halfway point; in the *quarter* roll pauses occurred at the top, bottom, and both sides of the roll. In the *snap* roll, the aircraft pulled up in midroll to pause in a near stall, then returned to its rolling course. Though other rolls were tightly turned, in the *barrel* roll the plane wove around in a larger orbit. In air combat, a roll right or left to the halfway point enabled the pilot to shift direction rapidly.

STALLS: The inexperienced pilot blundered into stalls early on. When flying speed slowed by climbing without adjusting the throttle (the hand-operated accelerator), the plane fell down backward, or to the side, until enough speed was picked up to resume normal flight at a lower altitude—but not too near the ground! Also, it was easy to slip off into a dangerous spin from the point of stall.

In the hands of the stunt pilot, stalls become eye-catching: *Hammerhead*—the pilot zooms steeply to the stall point, manages to turn out and dive back in reverse, or in another direction. *Whip*—the same zoom, but the pilot allows the plane to slide backward tail first in a curve to a level, pauses, then dives forward. If the plane is up to it, the dive may be pushed forward and under into upside-down flight (no Jennies need apply here), also called a *tail slide*. *Falling leaf*—the pilot guides the plane to slip sideways off the stall point in spectacular dips and swings to either side, like tumbling autumn leaves.

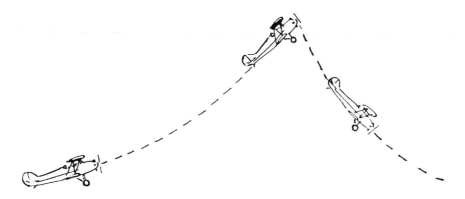

Stalling out; a deadly mistake near the ground.

REVERSES: These stunts were mostly invented in air combat situations. They were an abrupt means of shaking off enemy pursuit. The *wingover* reversed the plane's direction as suddenly as possible into a swift, shallow dive. The *Immelmann* started with a loop and at the top turned into a half roll to abruptly change direction. A *chandelle* was the sharpest climbing turn possible to near the stall point so as to be able to reverse direction.

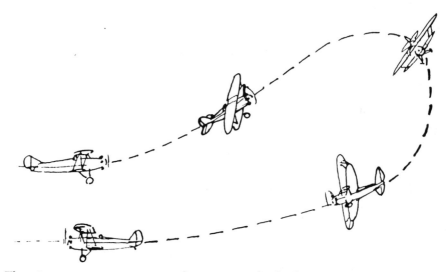

The wingover was a neat, spectacular way to get back where you came from.

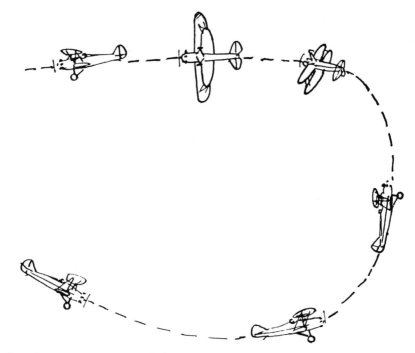

The Immelmann turn was named after an early German ace who wanted to get up and away from his pursuer (and maybe back down on that pilot's tail).

Also there was the *split "S"* maneuver, a half roll to position the plane for a steep dive. *Spins,* too, were fine spectator stunts, sometimes begun from upside-down flight, and perhaps ending in a grass-cutting dive when the pull-out fanned the lawn.

It was all showmanship and free in the early days before the big air "circus" organizations appeared. The gypsies in their Jennies learned that the lower, the closer to the spectators, they stunted, the more the gaping audience applauded. Probably the simple low-level pass or *buzz* was the most effective hair-raiser. No style, but personalized!

Down, around, around and around in the spin.

CHAPTER
4

Cow Pasture Businessmen

WHATEVER his stock of stunts and tricks, how did the barnstormer turn his aerial feats into a living?

At the beginning, it was easy because the barnstormer was a curiosity. Hundreds of towns had not yet seen a "daring young man in his flying machine." Often the aviator did not need to stunt. He appeared out of the blue, circled to attract attention, and landed in a convenient cow pasture. A crowd was sure to gather, and then it was up to the pilot's charm and smooth sales pitch.

Flying cross-country and stunting used up gasoline and parts. The gypsy pilot usually could not collect money for his air thrill show. He had to sell *rides* to earn his meals and lay cash by for the future. There might be a costly emergency at any time; or he might be saving to buy a newer, more powerful engine for his partner, Jenny.

A sort of friendly creature from outer space, the barnstormer offered rural people an adventure: Trust me, come fly with me! That was his pitch, but was he convincing? Could he persuade a half dozen or more local daredevils to part with five dollars for five minutes' flying time? Some benefitted from beginner's luck:

IN 1919, at the army's Mather Field near Sacramento, California, an enterprising flight instructor named McManus scrounged Jenny bits and pieces from warehouses and scrap piles to cheaply assemble a complete JN-4D. He intended this plane to be his sideline investment in the new barnstorming business. McManus had watched many student army fliers and picked a Norwegian-American, Birger Johnson,

Throughout the twenties Jenny was improved, as here at an Ohio plant, where she shows off new wings.

as his first choice to hire as his pilot. Johnson was bored in his postwar office job and was interested in the offer.

"What made you pick me out?" he asked.

"I noticed you might smear up yourself, but you didn't crash your ship!" McManus answered.

"I see."

"You bet. Too hard to get that Jenny pieced up ready to bring in the coin. I can get the crowds and the boys and girls who'll pay for a new thrill. You want to come in as pilot?"

"What is there in it?" Birger wanted to know.

"Five hundred a month and ten percent of the takings. One fellow has been at it already out here and he's doing fine. Besides the fares, there's county fairs. And carnivals. And civic pride. We can clean up, I tell you. How about it?"

"All right, I'll have a try at it."

A five minute thrill for a fiver. Ticket agent, barnstormer, and passenger are all smiles.

THE NORTHERN CALIFORNIA town of Sisson, on a flank of Mount Shasta, was selected as an early target. Sisson had never seen an airplane before, and excitement ran high. The mayor announced the day of the barnstormer's coming to be a general holiday.

Birger appeared on schedule and looked down with wonder and unease at the festive crowd. They covered his intended landing field and stood unmoving. In this forested mountain area there was no other nearby field. It wouldn't pay to stunt unless rides could be sold afterward. So the pilot repeatedly dived low attempting to disperse the spectators. But they in ignorance held their ground even as they wildly applauded his antics. Johnson sadly turned away, left behind the dollar-stuffed passengers, the mayor and his welcoming committee, and flying twelve miles north landed in a field beside the town of Weed.

When the crowd at Sisson learned of the flier's arrival at Weed, their curiosity to see the visiting marvel of the sky was so great that a couple of trains were chartered to go to the airplane! As the spectators closed in on the parked Jenny and its pilot, the silly questions began:

"I watched you, son, and I didn't see them wings flopping a gol-darn bit. And what happened to your feathers? All blown off?"

"Say, mister [pointing to the propellor], do you really need all that fan to keep your motor cool?"

"What is it that makes your ship run along the ground when you taxi? I can't see any gears or drive shafts, or clutches. How does the power get to the wheels?"

"Look here, you better come look at them wings of yours before you start to fly. I just found three holes in them, and I'll bet all your gas leaked out."

"S'pose you hit the top of a cloud, goin' that way more'n a mile a minute—wouldn't you blow them tires to hell-'n-gone?"

Despite the attention, Birger didn't clean up big bucks in Weed, California, due to a technicality: The mountain air was too thin to allow Jenny to lift a passenger!

However, during the six months that Johnson flew for McManus, the total money received amounted to $70,000. The pilot's share was about $10,000, so Birger Johnson bought a Jenny and went into business for himself.

BARNSTORMING profits from America's back country were mostly collected early on, for the novelty of paying to see and to ride with romantic young men appearing out of the sky soon faded. Later in the 1920s a gypsy pilot remarked: "The greatest danger in flying is starving to death." You could be a genuine wartime ace, or perform stunts that no one had yet seen, but if your ground publicity was poor then proceeds would be poor. The solitary, self-reliant pilot could make ends meet for a while by observing sensible guidelines and sales techniques.

Where? The level, open agricultural states lying in the nation's broad midsection were the main barnstormer territory, with sideshows in California and along the Atlantic seaboard. Jenny didn't like mountains or forested land without visible possible landing fields.

AERIAL WANDERER Leslie Miller secured a paying job for a few weeks flying publications between Jacksonville, Florida, and Atlanta, Georgia. Across the Florida border lay the massive, forbidding forest tangle of the Okefenokee Swamp. Miller respectfully flew around it at first, later experimented with short-cutting its edges. One day he set out straight across Okefenokee. Exactly at its center Jenny's motor stopped suddenly and never restarted.

Well, at least he was near maximum altitude, six thousand feet, but he knew he couldn't glide twenty miles. Finally Miller stalled and pancaked into a tiny open patch of bog, a soft splatter of a crash. Jenny would float there for a long time, but it was hopeless to hang around. No one would ever come to him; he would have to walk out. The pilot detached the cockpit compass and also an aileron (an eight-by-two-foot hinged flap on the edge of the wing) to use as a float and bridge.

Miller's hike was a horror of swamp wading; "sleeping" in trees; being bitten thousands of times by insects; stalked by alligators; looking a deadly water moccasin snake in the eye as it crawled across his stomach. Somehow he survived and maintained line-of-sight compass direction until on the third day, when, in a semidelirious state, he staggered and crawled onto a railroad embankment and managed with a final ounce of will to heave the aileron he still carried across the track before collapsing.

Sometime later a train, the Dixie Flyer, screeched to an emergency stop, discovered Miller, and carried him to a hospital, where, exhausted and gravely fevered, he remained for three weeks. A tough hombre, Leslie Miller secured another Jenny and resumed flying—but not over Okefenokee.

THE FURTHER into the country the barnstormer went, the better. The exhibition flier's dream was to uncover a county seat during its annual fair week. One that had never seen an airplane. Big bucks then, for sure!

When? A lot of barnstorming was seasonal (May to October). The far south was crowded in winter with fliers and not likely to be profitable to newcomers who didn't know the territory. Jenny was sheltered

The real guys for the right stuff 1920s style.

in a barn while her pilot worked at a winter job and tinkered with his airplane on weekends.

In drifting across the rural landscape, barnstormers soon learned that weekends were the best periods to sell rides. The climax of business came between two and five on Sunday afternoon. A take-off, five-minute circle, and landing cost the barnstormer around 50¢ in gasoline, so at $5.00 a passenger, a reasonably busy Sunday could provide a living in itself, outside of unexpected expenses.

Monday to Thursday might be spent on Jenny maintenance; or the knowing pilot visited the next town to set it up for his weekend: See about a pasture (try to get the farmer to settle for a ride and a small percentage of the ride earnings, making the farmer a natural publicist for the flier). Clear the visit with the town authorities, then tack up advertising and try to trade a free ride for local newspaper publicity. In planning ahead, the gypsy flier was always on the lookout for a special event—a fair or local celebration to join or locate nearby to stretch those primetime weekend ride hours.

Who? The fliers soon learned that country folk were the most willing and trusting prospects to buy a five-minute ride into the sky. Bystanders from big cities were more critical and cynical. Unsympathetically, some came out to see if the flying fool would kill himself today. When, after landing in some village pasture, the pilot stepped down from the cockpit, he claimed the full attention of the fast-gathering crowd. He needed to be considered as part mysterious, romantic hero, but also seem a nice guy whom you would trust with your life.

The rustics marveled at an outlandish flying suit, riding boots, aviator helmet and goggles, adorned perhaps by a casually trailing scarf (maybe a lady's silk stocking!). The dashing aviator had a line to go with his costume, and knowing the crowd wanted him to be one, easily claimed to be an ace, someone who had dueled with the Red Baron.

"Me an ace? Oh, yeah; I nailed eight huns. I flew with Eddie Rickenbacker as his wingman. Sure, he got twenty-six, but I didn't get there till October. The war didn't last long enough for me."

Maybe he hadn't finished flying school, but tall talking was part of his act and the audience expected and loved it. A sly character here or there took on an accent and stuck a monocle in his eye to pose as a *German* ace! A few real German aces did come over and perform with the big air circuses that formed later on.

To polish his nice-guy image, the barnstormer's checklist included being kindly and patient with children, dogs, and especially the many curious but ignorant questioners.

Kids were sure to be there and up front. So, smiling easily, he chatted nonchalantly with all of them, choosing one to be his helper and plane guard during the visit. He'd pay his assistant with a ride, maybe a loop, and a bit of hard cash. The kid did errands, helped service the Jenny and keep her clean, washed the cow dung off her underparts where the prop blast had sprayed it. Souvenir hunters were kept at bay and fools stopped from getting chopped in the whirling propellor. Plane guarding meant sleeping under the wing overnight if the flier stayed elsewhere. The animal world was interested in Jenny. Some cows craved the "dope," and a night's licking left wing and tail surfaces drooping in ruins. Also the Jenny was a refuge to wee animals who entered via the tail skid opening.

BARNSTORMER Basil Rowe took up an attractive young woman who appeared to be a calm type of passenger. Then suddenly she squirmed, shrieked, and climbed right out of the cockpit onto the lower wing like a practiced aerial acrobat!

"What's wrong?" yelled the startled pilot.

"Mouse!" she rippled back in the slipstream.

It took much shouted persuasion to convince her to trade the real danger of a five-hundred-foot freefall for the possible caress of a small rodent. Though she at length reentered the cockpit, the landing was made with her kneeling on the seat.

Rowe later received a white kitten stowaway via the same tail skid hole and made her his popular mascot. Famed air racer Roscoe Turner bought a lion cub for publicity purposes that grew into a much-photographed full-size front cockpit passenger.

DOGS? The barnstormer honored the rural adage that you could trust a stranger if your dog liked him. Dogs don't care where you part your hair, or about human financial or social status; of course, it's how you *smell.* The gypsy pilot, rich in the aroma of gasoline, castor oil, and likely not recently bathed, usually pleased the local mutts.

Some riders marched up tensely determined to get their daredevil aerial adventure over before they weakened. Others needed lots of persuasion and thereby went up relatively unafraid. A few of both types returned for rides and even wanted to pay to learn to fly. If a barnstormer found enough of these in one location, he might settle down and try being a "fixed-base operator" as long as he received enough paying customers. Many small town airports started that way.

Up in the air reactions varied. The rider, sitting in the forward cockpit, was in the pilot's view. Some passengers gazed down and

A Canadian Jenny up a tree.

around in quiet rapt attention. One treatment for nervousness was a bottle of whiskey, "liquid courage," sometimes also generously offered to the pilot. Violent air sickness had the pilot ducking, and his kid hosing out the cockpit before taking on another passenger.

It has been estimated that gypsy fliers, when things went well during the summer season, earned from $30 to $100 per week. But rain over several weekends; bad luck in working territory recently covered by another barnstormer; accidents—perhaps winding deep pasture grass round wheel axles during landing, causing drag that ended in a damaging nose-over or somersault—such misfortunes eventually clipped the wings of most single, truly independent barnstormers. As the twenties advanced, the players still in the game found it necessary to combine, and to add to their acts of aerial daredeviltry.

CHAPTER
5
I Was an Aerial Maniac!

MOST BARNSTORMERS realized, by 1923, that the public's attention to ordinary pilots and planes had faded. What did those fliers do who wished to carry on in exhibition flying?

BARNSTORMER Jimmie Mattern thought it was a good move when he rented a field across the highway from a tent-lined carnival midway. The crowd was ready-made. Jimmie, stunting above, could see walkers crossing from the carnival to look over this new attraction, and he made a fancy power dive landing approach to lure the gathering small crowd.

But this was outside Fresno, California, a medium-size city that had seen its share of aerial performers, and the selling pitch wasn't going well down below. Jimmie's assistant, Windy, was a better mechanic than salesman. He was sidetracked right off by a heckler who demanded proof of their Jenny's safety and kept it up until Windy blundered into telling about an emergency landing they had successfully handled a couple of days before.

That turned them off; nobody wanted to ride in a loser. A woman loudly announced that she wouldn't set foot in that crate for all the money in the world! The crowd sniggered and began to move off. Fresno was a zero in earnings for the men, and they were out-of-pocket for the landing-field rent.

But Jimmie and Windy were quick to understand their problem. After paying out the field rent, they walked over into the carnival grounds, bought hamburgers, and strolled slowly along the midway listening to the spiel of the tent show barkers. They agreed that the best-sounding hustler was a sideshow pitchman named Sport Carrington, and they propositioned him to join their team as promoter.

Sport bargained and cut himself this deal: He got the first one hundred dollars of income each week plus twenty percent of the team's profits. And most importantly, Sport agreed to provide a star performer for their barnstorming troupe. She was Trixie LaRue, high wire acrobat and Sport's wife, who would become the outfit's parachutist and wingwalker, making it a true air circus.

In his memoir *Cloud Country,* Jimmie Mattern describes Trixie as "a hail-fellow-well-met sort of girl, with an engaging smile and fearless eyes. Just how fearless she really was I learned in the hectic days that followed, days in which Sport's magic tongue rounded up customers by the dozen, and Trixie's daring wing-walking and jumping brought crowds milling around our landing fields."

The little air circus was a moneymaker while it lasted. Jimmie's personal share over seven weeks was two thousand dollars. But then it ended tragically. After about fifty successful jumps, the daredevil Trixie became increasingly careless. Jimmie was a very careful flier, so Trixie perversely teased his caution by disobeying instructions and leaping where and as she pleased.

On a day when there was a dangerous ground wind and it was

Jimmie Mattern: He quit
barnstorming after he lost
Trixie LaRue.

extra important to leap at the far upwind position, Trixie grinned mischievously at her pilot and jumped well before the proper time. She floated down into a railroad yard where the brisk wind hurled the unfortunate girl against a boxcar and she was knocked unconscious. At the hospital the grim diagnosis included a badly fractured leg, four broken ribs, and internal lung and other injuries.

Trixie's daredevil days were over, and so was the air circus, for Sport remained beside his wife during her long recuperation. Jimmie and Windy were back at their beginning. Personally shaken, Jimmie chose not to seek out new associates and quit barnstorming at this point, though not aviation. He became a Hollywood stunt pilot and later a famous long-distance flier.

THE BEGINNINGS of parachuting are far back in history. In about 1500, Leonardo da Vinci predicted and sketched an aerial umbrella. In 1797, Frenchman André-Jacques Garnerin designed and shaped a real parachute and went aloft with it dangling below a balloon. A huge crowd gathered to see if the aeronaut would kill himself in this novel fashion.

At six thousand feet Garnerin cut loose and made a colorful, slow descent. Because the parachute canopy had not been slitted to reduce air compression, the chute swung wildly as it spilled air, and the brave Garnerin may have been the first airman to become airsick as he entered the book of aerial records.

Thereafter balloonists kept a parachute handy, but aviators did not regularly carry them until well into the 1920s. In a senseless display of bravado, World War I combat pilots disdained to carry this life-saving gear. Scores of fliers leaping to avoid the agony of death aboard a flaming aircraft could have been saved by parachutes.

Exhibition parachutes during the early barnstorming years were often simply packed into a box set on the Jenny's lower wing. The jumper got into harness and either pulled out the canopy by the freefall plunge, or standing toward the wing tip tugged the parachute canopy into the slipstream, the rush of air currents passing the speeding aircraft, to billow and jerk the daredevil past the tail into air space (Trixie's method).

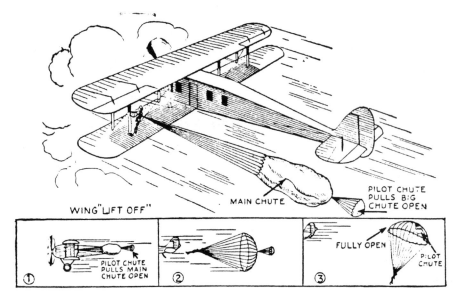

The "wing lift-off" method of leaving the plane with a chute.

Becoming an aerial jumper was a way into aviation for the eager amateur without funds or flight training. The routine required little instruction, just courage. Though parachutists often later became fliers, pilots usually shied at adding chuting to their skills. Therefore the beginning exhibition jumper could earn good money during the years when the parachuting fad was a crowd-pleaser. Famed round-the-world flier Wiley Post got his start as a jumper.

WILEY WAS an Oklahoma oil-field worker who often looked into the sky with longing when the Jennies of the barnstormers crossed overhead. In 1924 Post made his most important decision. He quit his job and went to the nearby town where a two-Jenny air circus had stopped. I'll do anything to fly, he told them, but the barnstormers didn't need him. Wiley hung around anyhow.

The air circus daredevil jumped three times that week and during the third landing injured his ankle. So there was Wiley, volunteering to leap in his place. The boss pilot was suspicious that this greenhorn would chicken out up in the sky and be carried back to the field, having had a free ride. Post pleaded, offered to do his first jump free, and so it was agreed. The amateur went up and jumped from two thousand feet:

Suddenly all motion stopped. I seemed to be floating in the
air. The plane was gone. I did not have the sensation of
falling I had anticipated. With a sharp jerk the parachute
opened. I looked up and saw it spread out above me. I
grabbed the old "shroud ring" made from the steering wheel
of an automobile. While still hanging tight to the ring, I first
felt the sinking sensation. I swallowed hard and for the first
time looked straight down. That was one of the biggest thrills
of my life. The people below looked like so many ants and the
fields like brown or green carpets. Gradually things took
shape. I guess it didn't take more than two minutes for the
drop, but to me it seemed like a couple of hours. I never saw
so much that stuck in my memory in so short a time.

Wiley bent his knees and landed neatly in the soft furrows of a
plowed field, turned as he'd been told to do in the direction of the
still-blowing canopy, and was jerked forward into a crash landing on
his nose.

The next time he leaped for the same circus he received fifty

Wiley Post: Here plump and prosperous in his prime as a round-the-world flier.

dollars. Before long the confident Post raised his jump price to one hundred dollars, more than a two-Jenny outfit would pay. Then Wiley promoted himself as a self-employed daredevil. He contacted the chambers of commerce in prairie towns, offering to highlight civic celebrations, popular in the 1920s, with his special appearance and parachute jump. Wiley asked and received up to two hundred dollars. His profit was tidy because he hired his ride over the jump site from a local pilot for about twenty-five dollars.

At the height (or plunge) of his success, Wiley arranged to do his death-defying act over his hometown of Maysville, Oklahoma. Carrying his chute under an arm, he turned up on his parents' doorstep to stay the night before the performance. He'd hoped they would be proud of him, but instead they reacted in fear and embarrassment for their wandering son. When Wiley awoke in the morning, he discovered that his parachute had disappeared! Suspicion surely pointed toward Mom and Dad, but after their smooth-faced denials, what could he do? The missing chute never did show up.

Now it was Wiley Post who suffered the embarrassment of cancelling in front of friends who might think that he was a phony. But Wiley rescheduled for the following weekend, bought another chute, and took care to base himself in the next town. On Sunday he flew over and parachuted professionally as Maysville's own aerial adventurer—and ate a chicken dinner with his parents.

A CHILDHOOD DAREDEVIL urge is evident in the backgrounds of some outside-the-cockpit aerial performers. Thomas S. Baldwin, the veteran balloon showman and parachutist (from 1880) who trained Lincoln Beachey, was taken on by a circus promoter who saw him as a fourteen-year-old railroad brakeman doing handstands atop a freight train rumbling through town. Arthur Starnes, long-lasting aerial performer, did similar tricks as a youngster high on steel beams at his father's construction sites.

Flying an airplane no longer thrilled Al Wilson, an instructor pilot. Bored by riding with a competent student pilot, Wilson would climb out and sit on a wing "to cool off." So he became a plane-change specialist. A similar restlessness provoked a tall, twenty-six-year-old Texan, Lieutenant Ormer Locklear of the U.S. Air Service, to become, by 1919, the most famous of the wing-walking pioneers.

WHILE STILL an army air cadet, Locklear wanted to escape the confinement of the cockpit. The first time he tried was during a test in which he, as a student pilot, was to write out in the air a word message flashed at him from the ground (no radio yet). But the lower wing nearly always obscured part of message. Ormer, leaving plane control to his nervous instructor, was inspired to crawl out and down to sit on Jenny's sturdy landing gear spread bar and there recorded a perfect score.

On another flight with an instructor along at the dual controls. Jenny's radiator cap vibrated free and the cadet daredevil braved scalding splatters as he wriggled forward onto the nose and carefully

Ormer Locklear tail-sits patient Jenny as a companion pilots her in the (obscured) front cockpit.

"Like leaning against a brick wall." Ormer Locklear does his stuff.

stretched between the pounding rocker arms to rescrew the cap just behind the whirling propellor. Another Jenny, on a separate occasion, offered a loose sparkplug wire. Ormer reconnected it by standing on the leading edge of the wing support in the full prop blast and leaning riskily against the vibrating side of the engine mount.

This was neat!—and Locklear wanted more air thrills. He prowled the wings; there were a lot of struts and brace wires to grasp between the Jenny's wings, but topside was smooth and scary even if there were foothold strut wires looping through from below. Ormer climbed on top, crouched there awhile, then confidently stood up into the seventy-mile-per-hour wind. He said it was like leaning against a brick wall!

Soon he had done all the bizarre, dangerous stunts that could be done on one plane: crawl back and sit on the tail, hang inverted from the landing gear spread bar or from Jenny's skid loop below the wing tip, do hand stands on the top wing. No parachute, ever. It all became crazily routine to Lieutenant Ormer Locklear.

Of course, his commanding officer found out, but Colonel Tom Turner's reaction, finally, was to use the Air Service's incurable daredevil for publicity purposes. That decision ended Locklear's other ambition—to go and fight in the air war over the Western Front. So, still restless, the official aerial maniac pushed on to the ultimate feat: plane-changing—to go up in one plane and come down in another.

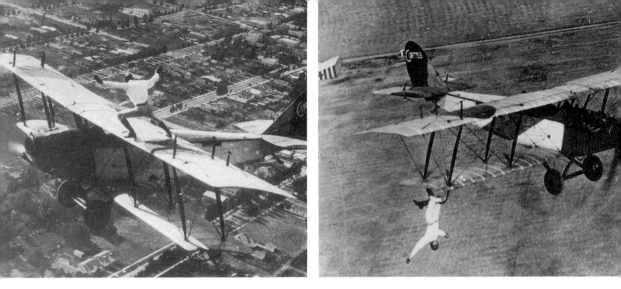

Plane-changer Al Wilson has written that, before rope ladders were introduced, it was easier to climb up to another plane than to drop down to the one below. In ascending, the plane-changer stood toward the tip of the top wing, grasped the lower wing skid loop brought within reach by the skill of the pilot, and climbed over onto the wing and so to the cockpit. Descending was more chancy, dangling and then leaping, *just so,* onto the bare upper wing. Ormer in his historic first plane change did it the hard way.

Sitting on the wheel axle spread bar, he depended as always upon the sure-handedness of his pilots, Lieutenants Elliott and Short. The second plane rose close below, risking a spot of air turbulence that could fatally sandwich the aircraft. Ormer swung from the bar, watched the shifting of position and distance in the five- or six-foot gap, and dropped catlike on all fours on Jenny's top wing without puncturing it. The precision of the three aerial stuntmen kept Locklear a survivor.

Enter William H. Pickens, the greatest press agent and daredevil promoter of the times. He had managed many early fliers, including Lincoln Beachey, and at one time had accumulated fifty-four airplanes, six flying boats, and a few blimps. He masterminded two mock attacks on Washington, D.C., as war preparedness publicity stunts. The very practical Pickens saw in Ormer Locklear, now leaving the U.S. Air Service, another gold mine in the sky and rushed to claim him.

Locklear and his associates contracted for fame and fortune, and

Locklear flanked by superb pilot assistants Elliott and Short, whose sure touch at the controls of the cooperating JN-4Ds made his act easier.

along the way found Pickens to be an exacting manager. He was fond of repeating that the five saddest words in show business were: "The management regrets to announce . . ." So Pickens wrote into contracts that his air circus would never postpone a performance. After Locklear was scraped and bruised in a botched auto-to-plane change, Pickens coolly reminded Ormer:

". . . Don't forget that we're both capitalizing on sudden death.

A Flying Circus poster depicts complicated two-way plane changes.

Changing Planes in Mid-Air

LIEUT. ORMER
LOCKLEAR
FLYING CIRCUS

Direction: WM. H. PICKENS
Stratford Hotel, - - Chicago.

And bandages are box office. They hold the romance of freshly healed accidents and the lure of catastrophes yet to come."

In the bigtime exhibition circuit of major cities and state fairs, the fee per performance was $3,000 (half to Pickens). Then Pickens landed a contract to have Locklear star in an airplane movie!

But it was all over for Ormer Locklear very soon. In 1920 he was killed in Hollywood, not wing-walking, but piloting a plane spiraling down a searchlight beam while ablaze with fireworks. Probably the flaring chemicals of the fireworks cut vital control wires. Locklear's funeral was a lavish publicity spectacle for the movie, now being rushed into distribution before the fickle public forgot who Locklear had been. William H. Pickens did not attend; he was busy signing a replacement aerial daredevil.

Ormer Locklear performing over a Milwaukee country club.

CHAPTER

6

"Slim" Lindbergh's Barnstorming Years

AS A RURAL Minnesota teenager, Charles A. Lindbergh, Jr., longed to fly for Uncle Sam and shoot down enough German planes over the Western Front to become an ace. But he was only sixteen when the war ended and had to shelve that dream. So Charles took up the closest activity to flying that was within his reach. He obtained a motorcycle and became a tearing daredevil upon the country roads of his neighborhood.

Lindbergh's parents had been separated for years, and he did not grow up closely influenced by his congressman father. Charles Jr., an only child, remained with his mother, and for many years he would judge the outside world by memories and standards absorbed from her.

So it was that when Charles began at the University of Wisconsin, his mother went along, and they lived together near the campus.

College seemed dull, so in early 1922, age twenty, Lindbergh turned back to his teen daydream. He got on his motorcycle and set off for Lincoln, Nebraska, to attend a flying school. Mother didn't approve of Charles becoming an aviator (but decided not to say so), so her son went on to Lincoln alone.

But the flying school turned out to be less than expected. Lindbergh's instructor, Ira Biffle, had recently lost some of his nerve and much of his interest in flying after the death of his closest friend in an airplane crash. He was gruff and distant in manner, often postponed lessons, or failed to show up as agreed. But "Slim" (as Lindbergh was called at the flying school and long afterward) was such a natural as a flyer that he learned a great deal anyway. When Biffle suddenly announced he was leaving his job, the deft student boldly asked the school manager for permission to solo.

However, the flying school was nearly broke and had sold planes to raise money, including the one in which Lindbergh had practiced. The new owner demanded a five-hundred-dollar "damage deposit" for use of a plane, which Lindbergh didn't have. His flying career was wobbling off the runway. So Slim pleaded with E. G. Bahl, the barnstormer who had bought "his" airplane. Could he go along as a helper? Bahl said in a kindly way that he managed okay on his own. Lind-

Charles Lindbergh as a speedy Minnesota teenager.

bergh, persisting, offered to pay his own expenses and work for free.

Slim was accepted, and the month he spent with the experienced barnstormer roaming the small towns of Nebraska gave him a modest start in practical air-show work. He did the chores—servicing the aircraft, selling ride tickets, pulling the propeller through to start the engine—well enough so that his pilot began paying him. And Slim did a bit of wing-walking, too; edging out to stand between the wingtips as a come-on when the plane swooped low over some country town. He was getting started as a daredevil.

Back at Lincoln, Slim met the Hardins, a husband-and-wife parachute and wing-walking exhibition team that was based in Lincoln. When not doing their aerial shows in the area, Mr. and Mrs. Hardin fashioned and sewed parachutes for sale. Slim, acting on a personal vow to become a fearless parachutist, approached the couple and said that he needed *two* chutes.

"I want to jump—and I'd like to make it a double jump."

"A double jump? You want to do a double jump the *first* time?"

The Hardins were surprised but, yes, if that was what he wanted, it wasn't that much more dangerous. It could be easily managed, assured Charlie Hardin, for parachuting was certainly safe. That was why he was in the business of manufacturing these lifesavers that every pilot should carry.

Lindbergh secured a pilot and plane, went up and jumped. The first chute opened promptly with a satisfying CRACK! and Slim experienced the surge of ecstasy, of self-confident action that he had hoped for. Then he cut the tie to the protective canopy and freefell again, awaiting the next CRACK! It was a long time coming because the second chute had been shoddily packed. Even cool, purposeful Slim became alarmed in the rushing seconds. The canopy opened at last and Lindbergh wasn't even injured in the hard landing that followed.

That jump did it—in his own estimation Lindbergh crossed from yearning boyhood to confident manhood in the exacting craft of aeronautics. And he had gained a position of respect at the airport. Slim had observed with envy how people would point to an individual and reverently murmur: He's a *pilot.* Lindbergh noted with satisfaction that he was now singled out as the *parachutist.* Daredevils were ever in demand in barnstorming days, and soon Slim was asked by a gypsy pilot to come along with him for the balance of that summer as principal jumper and wingwalker.

The plane was owned as an investment by a rancher, "Banty" Rogers, the pilot was easy-going but sharp "Cupid" Lynch, and a dog named Booster rode along, too. Booster, fearless in the air, flew harnessed in an exposed straddle position just behind the pilot. The dog had the best view on the plane. During a landing approach, Booster might spot a jackrabbit skittering away below and, not understanding altitude, would struggle to attempt a fifty-foot jump in pursuit.

The barnstormer's route passed westward through Kansas, Nebraska, Wyoming, ending in Montana. Slim, now billed as Daredevil Lindbergh, capably performed his death-defying routine. First a stroll between the wings, then climb on top, stand up, and remain so as Lynch put the plane through an inside loop! Afterward, casually tumble off the wing, freefall, blossom, and land as a successful parachutist.

He craved the adventure of it, but Lindbergh also approached the stunts from a careful engineering point of view and believed nearly all danger was removed. Walking between the wings was easy with a strut or wire always at hand. On the top wing his feet were firmly set in clamps. He might fall stooping onto the wing (as he did in the loop), but he couldn't fall *off.* Because he was an all-in-one aerial daredevil, he carried a parachute anyway. And it would always open, he reasoned, if properly packed.

Remnants of "wild west" attitudes lingered in the range and mountain areas. At Red Lodge, Montana, a wealthy old rancher sped up in a big, open touring automobile, braked in a cloud of dust, swaggered over, and bought a ten-dollar trip over town. Just so it included a low pass up Main Street, he said. As they buzzed over the downtown storefronts, the passenger abruptly produced two six-shooters and, blazing away, emptied them to either side! Turning back toward flabbergasted pilot Lynch, he roared with laughter.

"I shot this town up a 'foot," he yelled back via the slipstream, "an' I shot this town up a 'hossback, an' now I shot this town up from a airplane!"

In the Western states lived tough people who had met danger at every turn. But doing stunts in the sky, and jumping from a plane were feats of daring they hadn't imagined. So they applauded and honored Slim, and Lindbergh was pleased with his first helpings of hero worship.

Slim spent that winter in Minnesota convincing his father of his two aims. First, he was determined upon an aviation career. He wanted to become an airline pilot, as soon as there were airlines. Second, he must practice his skills in his own airplane, he argued. He could make a go of it next season as a barnstormer. At winter's end, Slim's father cosigned the bank's loan to Charles Jr. of nine hundred dollars. Lindbergh went down to Souther Field, Georgia, in April of 1923 and bought a Jenny with a new OX-5 engine from the army for five hundred dollars.

Now Slim had a little problem. He hadn't soloed! Oh, he'd had a lot of offhand instruction and stick time with the barnstormers, but he had not flown alone. Of course he didn't tell the army that. Anyway, pilot's licenses were still only honorary certificates put out by flying clubs. Anybody could fly, or try to. Another complication was that nearly all of Slim's experience had been in Standards, the most popular barnstormer biplane after the Jenny. Slim went into the hangar and self-consciously looked over his JN-4D, trying to appear casual. He succeeded, for the chief mechanic checked him out and helped push the plane onto the flight line.

Souther Field was plenty roomy, so the student pilot taxied out and practiced rolling along the runway just up to take-off speed, then throttling back. Turn around and practice again, until the tryout, when he overdid it right into the air! Slim cut back the throttle immediately, landed hard on one wheel and a wing skid nearly wrecking the Jenny. Cheeks burning with embarrassment, he taxied back to the flight line.

Here appeared a good Samaritan, a pilot named Henderson. He allowed that maybe Lindbergh was a little rusty from not flying during the winter. Diplomatically, Henderson said that he had free time and offered to fly along a few times. This he did skillfully and assured Slim afterward that he could manage on his own. So encouraged and

"Slim" Lindbergh and pal just before he left barnstorming to become an army flier.

tutored, the student was able to decently solo in the quiet air of late afternoon the same day.

Lindbergh bounced around Souther Field until he had about five solo hours, then felt able to begin his planned barnstorming trip back to Minnesota by way of Texas. Just about every pilot Slim had met talked about flying in Texas, and he wanted that experience, too. The new barnstormer was warned that pilots avoided the South's midsection; too many swamps and rough, forested land. He was told to detour along the Gulf Coast.

But Slim thought he'd like to look over the bad territory. An extra fuel tank had been put aboard, giving him four hours' flying time. He was confident, so assured that though the army had supplied a compass, Slim hadn't set it into the cockpit panel yet. All went well on the first day as Lindbergh proceeded straight west as far as a pasture at Meridian, Mississippi.

The next morning, as Slim was preparing to fly on, "a wartime pilot" offered a five-dollar bill in exchange for a ride, and Lindbergh accepted his first passenger. He was a heavy fellow, and the take-off from the muddy pasture barely cleared the fence. Then it was a continuing struggle to keep from brushing treetops on the hillside beyond. Fortunately the Jenny made it and skimmed over the hill crest to get more air space between itself and the ground.

Embarrassed by the shoddy take-off, Slim gave his passenger a long ride as they chased an amazed turkey buzzard round the sky. After landing, the passenger praised their near miss over the treetops; just like he used to fly, he agreed. Then the fibber rushed off to tell everyone about his *first* airplane ride. That's how it was during most of the Roaring Twenties; you could learn a bit about flying today, and carry up passengers tomorrow.

Shortly afterward, Lindbergh took off for Texas, maneuvering around increasing showers. He was looking for a Mississippi River crossing, but the landscape continued solid and ever wilder. The storm clouds were thickening, too, and Jenny was too delicate to fight with a mean thunderhead. Slim spiraled down and landed in a rare open pasture. As he was taxiing, Jenny's nose plunged as the wheels entered a hidden ditch and the wooden propellor splintered.

Where was he? In Louisiana somewhere, he supposed. No, on-lookers told him; this was Mississippi. The future transatlantic navigator was lost. Lindbergh believed he was flying *west,* but had settled one hundred miles *north* of Meridian. The compass immediately became a permanent part of Jenny!

The area around Maben, Mississippi, was too isolated to have attracted a gypsy flier, and after the replacement propellor arrived, Slim pocketed a profit of two hundred fifty dollars from adventurous local passengers. The barnstormer flew on, barely crossing into Texas before moving northward via Lincoln, Nebraska, his aviation hometown, on into Minnesota to the town of Shakopee, where his father was that day campaigning for governor.

A cloudburst covered Shakopee, and as Lindbergh circled low around nearby Savage, Jenny's rain-drenched motor quit and the pilot had to come down immediately. It was into a marsh and the plane flipped over, again, remarkably, with light damage. Slim was several minutes getting loose without cracking his neck from his upside-down position.

The crash landing had been excitedly observed from a distance by two small boys who raced into Savage to tell that "an aviator had

"Slim" Lindbergh in his barnstorming outfit.

landed upside down in the swamp" and that they had "gone up and felt his neck and that it was stiff and he was stone dead!"

Immediately, almost everyone in town crawled and waded through the swamp to view this chance tragic thrill. They wound up helping to move the Jenny to firm ground, supervised by the "stone dead" pilot.

Charles Jr. assisted his father in his failing political campaign by flying him from place to place until the day of a minor crash on take-off. Charles Sr. bashed face first into the cockpit front, emerged bloodied and with smashed glasses. Thereafter, Slim returned to barnstorming in the region.

Slim was handsome, personable, and surely would have been handed the key to small-town hearts had he been interested. But in passing through he took no local girl seriously, and he didn't favor fooling around. Nor did Lindbergh smoke, or drink liquor, beer, or coffee. In his methodical way, Slim had tested each of these stimulants and depressants, then discarded them as weakening to body and character. He probably spent more time with his Jenny and related barnstorming chores than most pilots, and in the quiet of a hotel room he maintained a chart of sixty-five character traits, grading himself on such qualities as alertness, ambition, concentration, honesty, manliness, orderliness.

In late August Slim invited his mother to visit, and she came to Janesville, Minnesota, and accompanied Charles Jr. on a ten-day barnstorming tour.

Then Slim wandered down to St. Louis, sold his Jenny, and hung around employed in flight instruction. He had applied for the Army Air Service (all that up-to-date flying, free!) and moved a big step into his solid flying career when he was accepted for the class of Army Air Cadets set for March 1924. In the meantime, Lindbergh accompanied Leon Klink, an inexperienced pilot who had purchased a plane, on a typical barnstorming junket down to Florida and out near San Antonio, Texas, where two colorful crashes on take-off ended the adventure. Slim, uninjured as usual, reported to Brooks Field, Texas, for army air training duty.

CHAPTER

7

Air Stunts: Can They Top This?

I can not do the old things now
  That I've been used to do.
I'm all smashed up from doing stunts
  And so must keep from view.
In doing tailspins near the ground,
  I lost my nerve for sport.
I am not good for anything—
  One leg's a trifle short . . .

BARNSTORMER Leslie Miller, who had landed in the Okefenokee Swamp, was sitting, unemployed, in a Louisiana town. The flier had to do something to stir up interest. Well, there was a big bridge here over the river; what if he got some publicity and skimmed under it? When Miller told the local editor about his scheme, he was turned down with a yawn. Someone had done that already. Leslie knew he was about to be shown the door, so he desperately proposed:

"Well, I can top that. I'll loop the bridge!"

"Now you are shouting," declared the editor with enthusiasm, "but can you do it? Hmmm, we'll make the fee conditional on your success."

The event was set for Saturday. Miller would receive five hundred dollars if he succeeded well enough to be able to collect.

For the "loop king," the newspaper rolled out publicity, raked in advertising. By Friday they saw the campaign was effective, so for an additional fifty dollars Miller agreed to "fail" on Saturday and do the real thing before the certainly larger crowd that would gather on Sunday to see him fail fatally. The pilot was grateful for Saturday's partial practice flight because Miller knew he wasn't really that skilled at stunt flying.

At noon on Saturday most of the townsfolk were at either end of the bridge, with some show-offs standing on the structure, risking their lives if the plane hit it. From a thousand feet, Miller dove into the seventy-by-ninety-foot slot between the bridge and the water, passed through, climbed, cut throttle thereby causing a stall, and as the crowd gasped, slid off side-slipping nearly into the river. Then Miller landed and proclaimed his intent of succeeding tomorrow, or bust!

A huge crowd was there on Sunday expecting the barnstormer to bust in spectacular fashion:

> . . . The crowd was waiting, and as I now had my altitude it was either back out or start the dive, so I dove. Down I went with the throttle wide open all the way, doubt lurking in my mind meanwhile as to whether the wings would stand the terrific speed, and if so, would they stand the strain when I leveled off at the water to go under the bridge.

> It only took seconds to make the trip to the water and I swore that if I succeeded it would be the last time I would pull that stunt . . .

> I made it under the bridge, then straight up, as far as I dare go, now over on my back and holding her upside down I looked to see how far the bridge was below me. This action allowed the motor to foul up and to save it I had to get the nose down and dive for speed and control.

> When I had succeeded in starting the dive I was in much better position to gauge my distance than when upside down and I saw I was in excellent position to complete a perfect loop by again passing under the bridge.

> This I did and headed for the flying field to sit down and think of what a fool I had been. Just then I was determined to quit a business which required such violent action in order to

gain a livelihood . . . Sometimes even optimists have the
blues.

It was true; sensible flying and ordinary stunting were not enough
anymore. The pilot now had to regularly come up with a new aerial
trick—spectacular and dangerous. Then if the crowd applauded,
there was no rest for the aerial daredevil. Before coming around to
the same audience, another new stunt must be produced. For a few
years in the later 1920s, this reckless creativity introduced a wave of
feats of aerial daredeviltry, particularly when a movie camera could
be pointed to record the nonsense close up.

For example; what could be done with trains? Well, land on them,
take off from them. A fast train on a straight track with an empty
flatcar back some distance from the locomotive could be landed on
neatly. Jenny's minimum flying speed was forty-five miles per hour,
so a parked plane with propellor already whirling could be blown into
lift-off from the top of a faster moving boxcar.

A daredevil drop from plane to railway coach top was about as
difficult as leaping onto another plane. Though the train on its track
was a reliable platform, there was air turbulence immediately above
a rushing train that made the operation chancy. In the simple but
eye-catching movie stories of the time, the rescuing hero might arrive
that way. Or the heroine, escaping from the villain in the coach,
climbed on top and, skirt billowing in the wind, seized the rope ladder
dangling from the hero's Jenny. With heart-stopping slips and sags she
slowly climbed to safety with her pilot sweetheart.

Other aerial maniacs were picked up from automobiles, motorcy-
cles, and speedboats. Climbing up the ladder afforded the crowd-
pleasing illusion that the performer was pulling the plane downward.
One fellow actually tried sprinting to the rope ladder hanging below
a slow-flying Jenny as it passed him. He caught hold but was forced
into such giant strides to keep up that he never reached the necessary
climbing boost and so had to let loose and roll and tumble for a
punishing distance. For a movie, super-daredevil Frank Clarke once
galloped an unflappable horse alongside an airplane on its take-off run

An auto to Jenny transfer successfully accomplished.

and, leaping onto it, foiled the villain's escape by straddling the long-suffering Jenny's tail!

Plane-changing? Try jumping down to the second plane with one arm tied back, or, in a cowboy outfit with hat strapped on, lassoing the wheel of the plane close above and appearing to pull it down to a handy position. The 13 Black Cats, a sharp, Hollywood-based outfit, charged one hundred dollars for an ordinary plane-change. Five hundred dollars was the price of a change from one *upside down* aircraft to a second inverted one. In a faked accident during a plane-change stunt, the apparent victim tumbled about four hundred feet before a thin unwinding cable (invisible to the crowd) jerked a hidden parachute into life-saving bloom.

Other variations included the first aerial refueling operation.

Though it was technically possible to do that by hose, that way was too dull and easy for an air show. Frank Hawks, another pilot destined for fame as a record setter in the 1930s, carried aloft aerial daredevil Wesley May who crouched on the top wing with a five-gallon gasoline can strapped to his back. Earl Daugherty in the second plane obligingly extended a wing tip to Wesley, and he staggered aboard, crossed to the Jenny's tank, and poured in his resupply. Wheel changing was also a fad for a little while. As a Jenny went through a performance before a crowd, off came a wheel! Someone would have to lug up a replacement, change aircraft, crawl down, and screw the wheel on.

It's possible that stunt ace Art Goebel devised the most delicate and dangerous plane-change feat. A daredevil, bound hand and foot, was laid on the Jenny's top wing before take-off and accompanied it into the air. Then Goebel approached in the second plane equipped with a steel hook below the lower wing tip. By maneuvering carefully, Goebel was able to snag the rope securely bound about the prisoner's feet and hoist him into the air, where, with supple contortions the daredevil, shedding his wrist bindings, managed to arch up and clasp the Jenny's wing skid, and so climb aboard.

Speedboat to plane changes were a specialty of Mabel Cody down in Florida.

Star daredevil Gladys Ingle of the 13 Black Cats hauls aloft a spare wheel, crawls under Jenny, and attaches it at two thousand feet.

These off-center weights and contortions on the aircraft's surfaces show how stable a plane Jenny was. Sure, pilot skill in countercontrolling was vital. But consider the cop and convict sketch that was played out aboard a Jenny placed on primitive automatic pilot (the controls locked in neutral, medium throttle): Frank Clarke in police uniform chased convict-striped Mark Campbell out onto one wing, pursued him beneath and across the landing gear to collar the prisoner on the other wing. Jenny pitched and yawed all right but didn't fall out of control. *No* hidden pilot in this skit.

Plane-changers fell to their death occasionally, or were sliced swinging into a propellor's arc. The luckiest aerial maniac must be Al Wilson. Over southern California, the veteran plane-changer misstepped off a wing for real and, chuteless, fall end over end. Fortunately, Frank Clarke was piloting below and behind, climbing toward the plane-change position. Instantly he dove and snapped out to intercept his partner after a fall of about fifty feet. The lucky fellow jammed head first into the sturdy Jenny's upper wing panel and stuck there. The landing was a bizarre sight but technically okay. Wilson kissed earth afterward.

The Jenny's top wing became a stage for strange activities: How about a lady walking her wolf on a leash? It was the animal that became nervous way up there in the sky. It dug in with its toenails and punctured the wing fabric, but did not panic. It was during the twenties that flagpole sitting was a fad, so an aerial daredevil installed a six-foot pole in the aircraft fuselage, extending up through the wing. The fearless daredevil climbed to the T-bar cross on top and, gripping it, balanced upside down in the breeze.

Gladys Ingle, flashy wingwalker and plane-changer for the 13 Black Cats, used the top wing for sporting events. She played pantomime tennis there, wing tip across to wing tip, with a fellow Cat. Or Gladys set up a target at the opposite wing tip and shot arrows into it from the other side. Ingle also performed an Annie Oakley act of standing near one wing tip with her back to the target. The markswoman peered into a hand-held mirror, held a rifle backward over her shoulder with the other hand, and squeezed off shots. *Popular Me-*

Early on in 1920, Clyde Pangborn misses his connection and bites the beach.

chanics reported that three of the four shots fired hit the target!

A beaverboard runway was laid across the top wing span so that the versatile Wesley May could roller skate or bicycle there. In one grandiose skit, a saloon table with two chairs was installed on the wing. On the table was secured a whiskey bottle and two glasses. A pair of cowpokes sat there playing cards. A quarrel started over cheating and soon there was a shoot-out! Off the wing toppled the plugged loser into a long freefall before his parachute opened.

Wingwalkers no longer needed to take off or land riding in a cockpit; they were on the top wing. The 13 Black Cats team would provide a daredevil to stand on each top wing through a loop maneuver for four hundred fifty dollars. Hanging from the wing skids or landing gear spread bar, performers snatched objects from persons on the ground. Others hung suspended clenching the rope end in their teeth (usually supported by a thin wire shoulder brace that onlookers could not see). One air circus advertised a specialty: Death drop—NO PARACHUTE! Aerial maniacs were dumped by a Jenny at close range into haystack cushions.

At Venice, California, a barnstormers' poker game was briefly halted to listen to the proposition of an Indian, Chief Whitefeather. Displaying his thick black braid of hair, the chief said that for fifty dollars a trip he'd wrap it around a landing gear spread bar and hang thus with arms folded. To test him, the boys hung him from a rafter for quite a while. Later he succeeded in the air, too. Frank Clarke figured big bucks could be obtained from a hair-care sponsor. But the chief liked parachuting, too, and was killed attempting a ten-chute cutaway jump. Parachute number six fouled, and Whitefeather plunged the rest of the way.

With the appearance of the rip cord, which allowed the chutist to set the canopy release enroute, deep drops became possible and spectacular. A colored smoke pot could mark the plunge by day, or powerful flashlights by night. One stalwart performer didn't pull the cord until seeing the ground in the flashlight beam! Ex-carnival escape artist Joe Campi was shut into a box, hauled aloft beneath a Jenny, and dropped. A parachute was supposed to support the box to give the prisoner time to emerge with his own chute. Nothing happened, the

Art Goebel: One of the
very best stunt fliers.

Some of the poker playing barnstormers who interviewed, and then hung up, Chief Whitefeather.

box fell faster! Inside, Campi kicked and lunged frantically, finally broke out and opened his chute barely in time to land hard and injured, but alive.

Standards rebuilt with 150 horsepower Hisso engines were popular because they could haul up to four persons in the front cockpit and were also adequate for air circus stunting. Parachutists often went up in Standards sharing the cockpit with someone from the crowd willing to pay twenty-five dollars to be there at the leap's moment of truth. While a professional would not dare to doublecross the circus management, an amateur who paid for the thrill of jumping might back out, or try to.

A New York City night club personality approached the barn-stormer Clarence Chamberlin (later a transatlantic flier) and asked the veteran pilot to set up an air show just for him. The entertainer was certain that enough of his fans would come out for an afternoon of stunts and rides to make the operation profitable for both the pilot and himself. To increase the appeal, the star told all his friends that he would climax the air show personally by making his first parachute jump. And he promised everyone that he would carry and play a saxophone all the way down.

So it was agreed, and on the show day all went forward success-fully until the moment of truth. The performer had decided to release the parachute canopy and be pulled off into the slipstream. There he stood, nervously out on a wing, holding the release cord and the saxophone, his beady eyes fixed on the pilot. Chamberlin signaled: Jump!

The showman released the canopy, but at the same time he changed his mind! As the billowing chute jerked at him he managed

Jumping from the door of a large plane, the pictures showing successive stages in a chute jump. Note pilot chute pulling the larger one open.

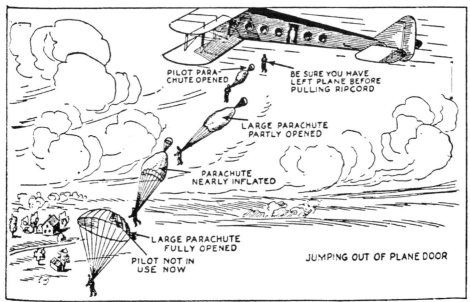

to wrap his arms around the outer wing strut, hanging onto the saxophone as well. The powerful drag of the open chute pulled the plane sideways. Something had to give! Not the jumper—he clung desperately. C-RR-A-CK! Suddenly he was gone; the strut had torn out of the wing! The famous personality floated peacefully above his cheering partisans, still clutching both the strut and the saxophone. He didn't play it, though, until quite near the ground, and then with just a weak bl-ee-aa-h sort of wail.

Upstairs, shocked pilot Chamberlain stared at the blank space where the strut had stood, felt a bad vibration, saw the top wing fluttering dangerously. The plane might disintegrate, and *he* had no parachute! Gingerly, the expert pilot side-slipped upon the strong wing side and babied the aircraft into a real emergency landing. Then Chamberlin set off to find a two-by-four brace to stabilize the wing for the flight home. Wrathfully, he hoped that two-by-four would come in handy to thump the "jumper" if he could find him!

Parachuting was exciting and paid very well if the wage were computed by the hour, but the repeated jolting of hard landings might permanently damage the daredevil: ". . . I'm all smashed up from doing stunts . . ." Here and there an exhibition jumper left a permanent imprint in the soil near some county fairground. Wesley May, one of the wildest aerial maniacs, came to an end as bizarre as any stunt he'd pulled in life. At the bottom of a routine jump May's chute drifted and snagged in a treetop. The tree stood in a cemetery. As Wesley was untangling himself, he suddenly slipped out and down, cracked his neck on a tombstone, and died.

CHAPTER

8

The Rescue of Rosalie

DID WOMEN participate in early aviation? Certainly; the Wright brothers had a sister. Katharine Wright had a close relationship with Wilbur and Orville, flew with them as a passenger, and became their business associate. But the record of women in the air goes back a hundred years before the Wrights.

Remember André-Jacques Garnerin, the inventor in 1797 of the parachute? His daughter became an exhibition jumper in the early 1800s. And there were several popular female balloonists during that century. After airplanes appeared, women pilots soon attracted notice. Harriet Quimby was a Manhattan publisher's assistant who became a stylish flier and entered aviation records by a solo trip across the English Channel in 1912. Ruth Law and Matilde Moisant were American pilots who starred in the air exhibition circuit in its most exciting and dangerous times before World War I.

Nineteen twelve was also the year that the first of the flying Stinson family of Alabama and Texas soloed. Twenty-one-year-old Katherine Stinson was a natural flier. She was the first female looper (over five hundred times), sometimes looping at night with fireworks attached to the aircraft to trace her course. A famed exhibition flier by 1915, she toured throughout America, then went on to Japan and China.

Katherine's sister, Marjorie, was taught by the Wrights and soloed at sixteen. Later their two younger brothers followed to become pilots—four early fliers from one family! The Stinson sisters were valued instructors of army air cadets during World War I. The principal

(Above) Harriet Quimby: The Manhattan secretary who flew over the English Channel in 1912. (Below) Adventurous air pioneer Kathy Stinson pilots a Wright Model B.

disappointment of Katherine Stinson's aviation career was that she could not obtain official permission to fly and fight over the Western Front.

Quimby died in a Boston air crash, but the Stinson sisters, Law, and Moisant survived the hazards of early flying days and retired. When Matilde Moisant announced her intention to quit, she was persuaded to make one more appearance with the air show, then at Wichita Falls, Texas. As Moisant was landing, spectators ran heedlessly into the way and the pilot, turning aside to avoid killing them, crashed the flimsy aircraft. Matilde was dragged out of the wreckage with her long skirts afire but lived to tell that story among many others.

In the twenties there were some women barnstormer pilots, not many, but skilled professionals. Ruth Law operated a flying circus in the Western states; Mabel Cody, who personally invented the speed-boat to aircraft change stunt, efficiently bossed her own outfit in the Southeast. Laura Bromwell, stunt flier, went up over Long Island one day in 1921 to see how many loops she could perform in her Standard.

Laura Bromwell: She performed 199 loops.

Laura started at 8,000 feet, looped repeatedly, gradually sinking to 4,000 feet. She climbed again to 6,000 feet, resumed looping with a will until her altitude was only 400 feet. She landed then and learned the official count was 199 loops. Bromwell was disappointed there were so few! Not scrambled by all her revolutions, she immediately took off and performed a full and varied stunt program.

Bessie Coleman, a Texas native who moved to Chicago and became a beautician, had a racial problem when in 1922 she aspired to become a flier. No American flying school would train a black woman. But Bessie persisted in trying and obtained a champion of her resolve in the editor of a black Chicago newspaper. She was encouraged to study French, and with that language, plus her savings, was able to go to Europe and be taught flying by accomplished instructors in France and Germany.

Returning to America, she obtained a promoter-manager and embarked on a national barnstorming career. She received many letters from black men who yearned to fly and were unable to obtain instruction. In 1926, reacting to their pleas, Coleman went to Florida to found her own flying school. But the black aviatrix was killed at Orlando, Florida, while riding as a passenger in a plane piloted by her white male assistant.

In the era of the air circuses, women were preferred when available as crowd pleasers in the aerial daredevil crafts of wing-walking and parachuting. Like Trixie LaRue, the ill-fated performer working with barnstormer Jimmie Mattern, most came into aerial daredeviltry from gymnast acts in show business. So it happened that a showgirl amateur became involved in one of the most publicized airborne crises of the 1920s.

Young, attractive Rosalie Gordon had done a bit of wing-walking with the Gates Air Circus, one of the largest operators, when it was working the Los Angeles area. When her parents found out, they persuaded her to give up the dangerous craft. Now, in February 1924, Rosalie was a chorus girl performing in a night club revue in Houston, Texas, when the Gates outfit came into town. On a whim she contacted Ivan Gates, and the savvy promoter employed Gordon to make

Black aviatrix Bessie Coleman.

a well-publicized first parachute jump, a local-girl-makes-good type of promotion.

About five thousand persons paid a dollar each to see the Sunday afternoon program of air thrills and stunts. Rosalie, Houston's own girl daredevil, the crowd favorite, was the final performer. She was stylishly clothed in a white jump suit, helmet, and boots adorned with big red buttons. If the petite daredevil had sprouted ears she could have been the Easter Bunny!

Clyde Pangborn, chief and veteran pilot for the air circus, knew that his fuel tank was less than half full, but ignored this because taking the chutist up and leaving her would take ten minutes or less. Also riding along was Milton Girton, circus aerial performer, who would assist Miss Gordon in getting set to jump.

The preparation was routine. The girl fearlessly climbed out and sat on the wing edge while Girton helped her with the parachute harness. The rope trailed beneath to the parachute pack attached below the spread bar between the wheels. This was to be a jump-and-pull parachute operation. Pangborn maneuvered to the proper position and signaled. Without hesitation Rosalie leaped.

She fell about twenty feet and was snubbed by a violent jerk. This was expected, but when Gordon looked up hopefully there was no canopy there! Well, at least she wasn't falling swiftly to extinction. The girl was hung up; her chute failed to emerge from its pack.

Girton reported the situation to pilot Pangborn, who directed the daredevil to go below and attempt to hoist Miss Gordon back to the plane. This may have been possible in the beginning had Rosalie climbed, too. But, windwhipped and swinging like a pendulum, Rosalie, in shock, was of no assistance. Girton labored without effect.

The crisis was apparent to the watchers on the ground, particularly other pilots. Several took off and flew nearby, lending moral but no physical support. Pangborn, after realizing Girton could not retrieve Rosalie, did some deep and desperate thinking—urged on by the plane's low fuel supply. Landing while trailing the parachutist would likely be fatal to her. Somehow, she had to be pulled up to the plane. Now if there were two . . .

Pang flew low over the airfield and the gasping crowd. He hurled a message wrapped in his helmet from the cockpit:

"Get Freddy Lund up here!"

Freddy Lund was a spectator among the crowd. But he had in the past been a first-class aerial performer for the Gates Circus, leaving with several others after a major quarrel with boss Ivan Gates. Lund was just out of a hospital, a convalescent from a recurring wartime injury. Yet he responded briskly and, with pilot Tommy Thompson in another Gates plane, was soon aloft near and below Pang's Standard trailing its helpless burden. Freddy stood up in the cockpit and dis-

The star of the Gates Flying Circus was always called Diavalo, so the company wouldn't have to waste posters when a performer had "bad luck."

played a knife. He motioned that he would stand on the upper wing, grasp Rosalie as she swung by, and cut the binding rope.

Pangborn replied with a vigorous no-no shake of head and inscribed a circle with a finger. Gordon was swinging unpredictably, could too easily enter the fatal arc of the second plane's whirling propellor. He signaled Lund to join them, to crouch beside Girton on the spread bar and help haul up the parachutist. Pilot Thompson edged into the delicate positioning for this plane-change, which was just barely accomplished. Lund was wearing dress boots with slick leather soles. In leaping down they slipped on the wing surface. Lund sprawled and nearly became a casualty himself!

Now Lund and Girton struggled together, but the rope had become slickened by oil occasionally spattering from the engine. They had no success, and Lund was in no shape to continue the effort for long. He crawled back on top and told Pangborn that he couldn't do it. But he was a pilot who could fly the plane while Pang, their last human resource, joined the rescue attempt.

Clyde Pangborn was tall, slim, and wiry, probably the strongest of the lot. He joined the weary Girton and together they pulled and made inch-by-inch progress. Those inches slowly lengthened to feet, and finally Rosalie, now fortunately revived, dangled just four or five feet below. Snubbing the rope firmly to the landing gear attachment, Pang lowered himself and shouted for Gordon to grasp a leg. The girl did so, then with a desperate lunge upward managed with her other hand to claw and grip her savior's trouser belt. One final heave by Pangborn and Girton and all three daredevils were perched on the Standard's sturdy spread bar!

Pangborn climbed back and exchanged cockpits with Lund. As he lifted his leaden arms to the controls, Pang knew it wasn't over yet. The gasoline gauge signaled zero though the engine still ran smoothly. Gordon was too exhausted to come topside, so the pair would remain on the spread bar. A perfect landing was required. Would the pair hang on in the jolts of contact? Would the wheel attachment hold, or would they be squashed in its collapse? Could they keep the parachute rope from snagging something?

The engine continued to run; the landing was precise; the wheel attachment held; the rope snagged and dragged at Gordon and Girton, but the crisscrossed piano wire braces held them aboard. As the Standard coasted to its glorious halt, the whooping crowd surged to envelop the plane. Milton Girton, survivor, had the presence of mind to yell out from underneath:

"Stop that engine! Do you want to kill somebody?"

Rescuers Pangborn, Girton, and Lund suffered rope burns on their hands. Pang additionally had a cheek laceration from bracing against the landing gear support wires during the struggle. Rosalie chatted volubly with newspaper reporters, laughed rather too easily. When a close friend rushed up, she collapsed into overdue tears. It was discovered that the parachute pack had been left outside during the previous rainy night. A check of the Standard's gasoline tank revealed that they had cut it pretty fine. Two or three minutes more and it would have been curtains!

The rescue of Rosalie was a great boost in publicity to the already thriving Gates Air Circus. It went on (without Miss Gordon) to carry more than two hundred thousand passengers per year in its aging aerial workhorses, eleven Standards and Jennies at its peak. Gatesman Bill Brooks claimed a daily record: nine hundred passengers carried

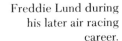
Freddie Lund during
his later air racing
career.

at one dollar each per very short hop. In the later years Ivan R. Gates and Clyde Pangborn became partners.

"Upside-down" (a stunt specialty) Pangborn was in charge of all aerial operations. Gates, no flier, was a cruder edition of the William H. Pickens breed of promotional genius. An exuberant individual, Van Gates had a hair-trigger temper. Like Pickens, Gates's attitude toward his performers was callous. When the tragic bad luck of some of his parachutists resulted in the wasting of batches of posters printed with their names, the boss thereafter identified all his aerial maniacs simply as "Diavolos" (devils).

Van was also an alcoholic who was violent when he was intoxicated. On one occasion he unexpectedly attacked Pang from behind. Pushed off, he produced a .45 caliber pistol and pointedly fired six shots within inches of his associate. That their business partnership survived this incident testifies both to the unflappable calm of Clyde Pangborn and to the flavor of business in the air circus trade!

The air circuses were big enough to stage spectaculars that ordinary gypsy pilots hadn't imagined. A Gates production sent a five-plane cavalcade through Manhattan, from the Battery north all the way up Broadway, sometimes below building levels. Wildly zooming, stunting, and alive with aerial maniacs standing, walking, hanging; the event was a sensation! At this time there were no laws governing such escapades. The *Evening Graphic,* a racy New York newspaper, sponsored and planned the event.

Other entertainments could be staged by any size air circus. With front cockpits in the Standards big enough to hold four, aerial weddings—minister, bride and groom, witness—became popular and provided excellent air circus publicity. At the "Jenny Scrambles" the pants race was a favorite. Several pilots dropped their trousers at a designated spot, ran in shorts to their Jennies, took off, made a tight circle, landed and taxied, jumped out and ran to be the first to struggle back into their pants! No zippers then; they had to contend with buttons.

The old-lady-in-distress routine started at least as far back as Linc Beachey. Let's use an example from an El Paso, Texas, army air show

GREETINGS!
From the Trans-Continental
GATES FLYING CIRCUS
of San Francisco, California.
("The Daddy of Them All")

Starting at the top and reading around the picture to the right are: Clyde E. ("Upsidedown") Pangborn, Chief Pilot; Ivan R. Gates, General Manager; "Big Jack" Ashcraft, Pilot; Eddie Brooks, Pilot; "Wild Bill" Wunderlich, Acrobat; George Daws, Director of Exploitation; Chance Walker, Pilot; Freddie Lund, Pilot; "Diavalo" A. F. Frantz, Chief Aerial Acrobat.

Members of the Gates Flying Circus and their specialties were featured in this garish promotion flyer.

in the twenties. Between stunting bouts, rides were being given. A chauffeured limousine half a block long pulled up haughtily beside an airplane. Out of it, with assistance, crept the richest, oldest lady ever seen—bent and gnarled, thin white hair, pearl necklaces drooping over ancient black satin. She vows she will fly before she dies!

The air showmen approach Mrs. Gotrocks with respect, slowly and gently boost the feeble passenger into the cockpit and adjust her safety belt. The propellor is pulled, the Hisso engine snorts, starts, and idles. Before boarding, the pilot walks to inspect a wing aileron. Everything must be in perfect order for the flight of the rich old lady!

Abruptly the engine roars, and with a jerk the airplane is on its way fish-tailing aimlessly out into the field leaving the pilot behind in wind-whipped dust. Prematurely, the old Jenny claws into the air as the helpless passenger's white locks flutter in the breeze. Down the aircraft bounces, hard, then somehow gets back into the air and goes tearing away low over the cactus.

Suddenly it takes a mind to climb again. But look! It's turning around . . . and now it's on its back . . . flips over again and dives straight at the crowd! They scatter like chickens before the assault of a hawk. The wild Jenny zooms, performs a chandelle, and at low altitude proceeds to do every stunt in the book, between menacing dives at the thoroughly frantic crowd. Wow! They are getting their money's worth.

The old lady crookedly approaches the field, one wing low, slips sideways almost into the ground. Bounce! Bounce again, and as the Jenny slows it crabs left, ending in the whirl of a safe ground loop. Then it taxies briskly to turn and halt before the wondering crowd.

Out hops the ancient dame, now tall and athletic, walking with springy step. The pilot bows, strips off his wig and is revealed as Lieutenant Claire Chennault, who before World War II would organize and lead the Flying Tigers in China.

Oh, the twenties were the heyday of crazy air thrills; but though the barnstormers weren't listening, from Washington, D.C., a message was blowing in the wind:

The old lady has had her day!

CHAPTER

9

Safe and Sane . . . Except in the Movies

SLATS RODGERS, a veteran Texas barnstormer who began his flying aboard a homemade airplane in 1914, was, ten years later, about to fly to an air show location. Entering his old Jenny's cockpit, he moved the ignition switch and heard a snap. It had broken in the *on* position, okay for starting up, but the motor could not be stopped completely without getting out and applying pliers to turn a valve at the carburetor. Well, okay, let's go anyway.

A wind-driven siren had been installed underneath to grab attention over the air show crowd. Once in the air, Slats tried it. The wail was loud and—because some part had loosened—continuous for hours since the pilot couldn't shut if off! Then Rodgers noticed that the 180 horsepower Hisso engine was running ever faster. He found he couldn't cut back the throttle because its control wire from the cockpit had disconnected!

So the loose Jenny arrived over its destination airfield in a hurry. Round and round the plane turned for an hour and ten minutes using up gasoline, siren screaming, while its captive pilot hoped that the wide-open engine wouldn't destroy itself. Finally it choked off, and Rodgers successfully guided the plane, siren now moaning low, into a dead-stick landing. But with the jolt of touching down, another dose of gasoline trickled into the carburetor (and the ignition remained on). With a snort the Hisso resumed roaring. No choice but to take off again!

Slats made a tight turn chancing that the motor would continue long enough and was safely in landing position when it again stopped.

This time the Jenny rolled powerless until its tail skid came down; then the rebel engine started sputtering again. Slats, leaping out, managed to grip a wing tip and hold on. The defiant Jenny turned around and around dragging the stubborn, clinging Rodgers as the engine stammered and the propellor windmilled. By the time help arrived the Hisso had finally run out of gas and given up. Into the silence a mechanic blurted:

"What's the matter?"

"*You* think of something that ain't the matter!"

Yes, the Jennies and Standards had become old and ramshackle. They had endured almost ten years of outside weather and casual maintenance. Some had been modified by installing the powerful Hispano-Suiza (Hisso) engine, roomier passenger cockpit, even improved wings. But the new parts were joined to an aging whole. Few new aircraft trickled into air exhibition activity during the free style stunt years. Why not?

In the early 1920s, the obvious surplus of cheaply available war aircraft did not encourage American manufacturers to produce new planes. Later, when air technology could deliver much better aircraft, the air circuses couldn't or wouldn't afford to buy them.

This lag suited the civil air establishment (the manufacturers, aeronautical engineers, wealthy amateurs) who had always looked down their noses at do-it-yourself air exhibition flying. Gypsy pilots and air circuses were seldom mentioned in the trade aviation magazines. The industry would not be sorry to see that sideshow of flying closed down in favor of safe and sane air travel.

The airplane began as an unbelieved marvel, next became a "fool killer," then a romantic but deadly weapon of war, and lately an aerial platform for ever zanier stunts and daredeviltry. But now technology was ready for the era when the airlines would overtake the railroads. If people were to look forward to travel in the new, enclosed, passenger planes, their attitude toward flying must be changed. They must be persuaded that flying is the most practical way to get quickly from point A to point B.

Safe and sane government regulation was proposed as the solu-

Aerial newsreel photographers prepare to go to work.

tion, controls that would promote the new airlines and restrict the old barnstorming. So the critics heavily attacked the most obvious shortcoming of stunt pilots and associated aerial maniacs—safety. On an average, about seventy persons were being killed in air crashes per year. About a quarter of these were stunters. The campaign to eliminate that statistic enlisted just about everyone in aviation who did not earn his living as a daredevil.

Even Charles A. Lindbergh, now part of the aviation establishment after his transatlantic flight, wrote in the *New York Times* about the necessity of government regulation: "Something must be done to check inexperienced stunt flying . . ." Had he forgotten "Daredevil Lindbergh" in his happy days as a learn-on-the-job wingwalker and parachute jumper out west? And what about happy-go-lucky "Slim," taking delivery in Georgia of a plane that he did not know how to fly? And soon carrying passengers in it! Middle age was overtaking aviation, and the Federal Air Commerce Act of 1926 was passed.

Afterward the barnstormers remembered: "We were fliers and we were free!" That meant that anyone could fly anything anywhere anytime with anybody. The Air Commerce Act put that freedom in the past tense.

Broadly, pilots must be licensed by being officially examined for competence and, periodically, for health. Of course, the licensed flier could be unlicensed for cause, and grounded. Air instruction was also licensed, with curriculum and student flight hours regulated. Aircraft were strictly examined for air-worthiness, then registered and marked for identity. Stunting near the ground or above populated areas and most forms of outside-the-cockpit aerial daredeviltry were severely restricted.

Gypsy pilots were shocked and disgruntled. Suddenly they had become the dinosaurs of aviation! Few wanted, or could afford, to comply with all these regulations and paperwork. Some rebels followed the old ways for years in the back country, where federal inspectors were rarely encountered. A few went south of the border to continue to fly as they pleased.

Due to slow start-up of enforcement, it was a year or two before the bite of regulation penetrated. In 1928 even the mighty Gates Air Circus bowed out. It had visited about five hundred cities and carried aloft more than half a million passengers. But the circus needed new planes and regulated air stunting didn't attract crowds. The on-the-spot thrill of personally seeing airplanes diving close by with aerial maniacs prancing and risking death had been ended.

Except in the movies. There, though the viewer knew the stunting to be a secondhand, carefully planned experience, the opportunity for comfortably eyeing the close-up action was great for stunts that would have been blurs or distant dots at an air circus show. Some of the daredevil thrills were as risky on film as in the flesh.

The 13 Black Cats organization was started in 1924 in Los Angeles. Originally there were but three black cats: Bon MacDougall,

Clowning for the newsreels.

Ken "Fronty" Nichols, and William "Spider" Matlock, local pilots who had linked together to improvise an air show when the expected performers hadn't shown up. Success expanded the band to a maximum of thirteen, held to that number to mock superstition. The daredevils worked wearing an emblem showing a sassy humped cat and the number 13.

The original trio of Cats got a publicity boost during an early air show date. Stanford and the University of Southern California were meeting in their annual football game. The plan was to fly over the stadium at halftime with a Cat standing out on either wing to hurl a football marked with each school's colors down into the spectators. But the Jenny's radiator burst at the critical moment and the plane sagged *into* the stadium bowl. The footballs were tossed (no perfect spirals) in a hurry, as wingwalkers Nichols and Matlock scrambled for the cockpit while the foaming Jenny, now roaring at full throttle,

Bon MacDougall, a founder of the 13 Black Cats, with paying passenger in a JN-4D.

staggered over the stadium rim "by inches" and dipped into an emergency landing at a nearby airport.

No one was more frightened than the three participating Cats, but nobody believed that! It was thought to be a deliberate stunt. Stern newspaper editorials deplored the risk to public safety, but the publicity brought a lot of daredevil business.

One reason the public believed that "anything goes" in the air was that movie-goers in the 1920s saw newsreels of zany stunts often planned and performed by the 13 Black Cats. Movie cameras in companion planes recorded outrageous thrill skits like the top wing Annie Oakley act and the barroom brawl described in Chapter Seven.

Twelve Cats were males, but Gladys Ingle was their balance as the stand-out female plane-changer and top wing exhibitionist. Gladys, without parachute, made more than three hundred plane changes without a slip, and retired to raise a family. In fact, during five years of creative aerial nonsense, the skilled Cats never lost a feline in action. However, in 1929 they too went out of business. The movie companies had by then stockpiled film showing every air stunt yet contrived and were now more interested in feature story aviation epics where stunt pilots were hired as studio employees. Federal regulation was also a factor. But in their time the 13 Black Cats was the classiest independent stunt outfit around.

However, in its passion for realism, movieland did invent a dead-end kind of stunter who in turn became a last-gasp marvel of barn-storming. During movie stunting, it was discovered that a cockpit could be armored, padded, and secured so that a professional plane-crasher could survive real crack-ups.

Eight of the 13 Black Cats.
Back row: Albert Johnson, Bon MacDougall, Art Goebel, Ken "Fronty" Nichols, Paul Richter Front row: Herb McClellan, Sam Greenwald, Spider Matlock

Captain F. F. Frakes, a "Jenny jerker" since 1919, saw these final days of barnstorming in plain terms: "Once you are considered a freak by the public, you'll be in demand by the show promoters. In this game you must continue to get freakier and freakier with each passing year or you will be a has-been in quick order."

So, on his own, Frakes began crashing planes before paying spectators in 1930. Nothing fancy, you understand; no dogfight preliminary; just bargain to buy some flying junk heap as cheaply as possible. Prepare it, then haul it into the air for its last quarter mile flight to crash into the ground, water, building . . . whatever. As survivor Frakes eased out of the wreckage, he'd strike a match to burn it for extra crowd effect. What a showman!

The Air Commerce Act enforcers got quite excited about this in the beginning and grounded Captain Frakes. But eventually they saw it his way: Crashing into a designated object at a safe distance from the crowd was risky solely to the pilot. Thereafter Frakes crashed all through the thirties: at state fairs, air race meets, and before newsreel cameras. That is, up to and including crash number ninety-nine, it is reported. Then the leery air showman quit his act while yet ahead and alive and took a job with a carnival.

Crashing for big bucks turned back air exhibition flying to its "fool-killer" days. There was no visible grace or skills, just the lurking crowd paying admission fees to see whether the daredevil would kill himself. And this is where old-time barnstormers dead-ended; crashed upon the scrap heap of history.

WAS THERE a long-range social gain from the antics of the barnstormers? Yes, these aerial daredevils carried their infectious enthusiasm for aviation—"I am a flier and free!"—to all parts of the United States. From the barnstormer ranks came many pioneer air transport pilots and most of the air record setters at racing and distance flying in the thirties. A fresh new generation of fliers emerged from the impressionable youths who gaped at the marvelous antics of the barnstormer breed.

"I am a flier and I am free!"
Farewell to the barnstormer...

A POPULAR BIBLIOGRAPHY

The Barnstormers and *Air Devils*. Don Dwiggins
These are the two best books I've seen on their subjects.

Barnstorming. Martin Caidin
Profiles engaging personalities and tells their tales.

Jenny Was No Lady. Jack R. Lincke
From soup to nuts about the JN-4D.

Stunt Flying in the Movies. Jim and Maxine Greenwood
Attractive and thorough review of the subject.

The Man Who Walked on Wings. Art Ronnie
Detailed, illustrated biography of Ormer Locklear.

Old Soggy No. 1. Hart Stilwell
The straight dope! Slats Rodgers tells
it as he saw it.

"Upside Down" Pangborn. Carl M. Cleveland
Biography of the chief pilot of the Gates Air Circus.

The Spirit of St. Louis. Charles A. Lindbergh
Autobiography set as reminiscing during the flight
to Paris.

Command the Horizon. Page Shamburger
Lush recreation of aviation nostalgia.

The 1975 movie *The Great Waldo Pepper*, starring Robert Redford,
appears on TV now and again. Though on the melancholy side, the
film faithfully depicts barnstorming.

NOTES

Epigraph   Slats Rodgers quoted in *Old Soggy No. 1*—Hart Stilwell (1954)

Chapter I   Lengthy excerpt is from an anonymous barnstormer's reminiscences as told to Charles Gilbert Reinhardt, "Gypsying the Jennies" *Saturday Evening Post,* January 9, 1926. Used by permission.

Chapter IV   Birger Johnson's reminiscences from
Pages 22-25   *The Far Horizon*—Henry Lanier (1933)

Chapter V   Excerpt from *Around The World In Eight Days*—
Page 35   Wiley Post and Harold Gatty (1931)

Chapter VII   Anonymous verse in *Literary Digest,* December
Page 51   8, 1923

Page 55, 56   Excerpt from *Handsprings for Hamburgers*—Leslie Miller (1929)

Chapter VIII   The perils of Rosalie are recalled in three sources: "A Miracle of the Air" by James Whittaker, *Wide World,* September 1924; *"Upside Down" Pangborn*—Carl M. Cleveland 1978; *Baling Wire, Chewing Gum and Guts*—Bill Rhode 1970

INDEX